Instant Pot Duo Crisp Air Fryer Cookbook

Easy and Delicious Instant Pot Air Fryer Crisp Recipes for Beginners and advanced user

[Grill Academy]

Table of Contents

Introduction

The air fryer lid is a fantastic accessory for your kitchen. It is easy to operate, store, and use. So, you won't find any trouble running it daily. Here are some features to help you better understand your appliance.

Benefits of the Instant Pot Air Fryer Lid

Smart and Versatile: There are six pre-sets on the lid that you can work with. Apart from air frying, it can help you bake, broil, roast, dehydrate, and reheat. So, almost everything can be done with the air fryer Lid and at lower costs than other similar appliances.

Save Space: Instead of using six different appliances, you can use just one. The air fryer lid sits perfectly on the Instant pot and can cook a whole lot of recipes with an excellent taste and perfect golden finish.

Two Lids, one Pot: Since you will only be getting the lid alone, you will have to use the Instant Pot that you already have. As the new lid is made as per the dimensions of limited models, you will have to check the compatible models.

Healthy Meals all day long: Instant Pot Pressure Cooking is excellent at making healthy meals. But when you add the Instant Pot Air Fryer Lid to it, everything changes you will get a whole new world of possibilities. Healthy food that, too, made quickly is something every kitchen needs.

Safety First: The air fryer lid won't start, or the lid won't show anything until and unless the lid is not locked in properly.

How Does It Work?

The Instant Pot Air Fryer Lid works its magic via the lid only. As everything is installed inside the lid, you must take special care of this part. Because without it, you won't be able to cook fresh food with a golden finish. What you need to do is simply detach the instant pot lid from the base and out in the air fryer basket. On top of it, you will use the new Instant Pot Air Fryer Lid and select the required function.

The best thing about using this attachment is that you can use your existing pot and need not buy a new pot for cooking. This saves money and time.

Within this lid, there is a heating mechanism and a fan. When heat is generated, it is distributed evenly throughout the pot. This allows the food to be cooked evenly from all sides. Although it is a good practice to change the sides, not doing so will not affect the cooking intensity of your food.

At the back end of the lid, you will find two vents, one is used to suck in the air, and the other is used to blow it out. This continuous in and out of the air also ensures a perfect blend of all the materials added.

Cooking Functions of the Instant Pot Air Fryer Lid

The 6 Smart Programs embedded in the air fryer also work based on this rapid and efficient air circulation. The importance of air circulation is that you can prepare your food without using oil. Also, these smart functions or pre-sets have pre-configured time and temperature settings. You only need to press the button and then press Start. And wait for the magic to happen. Even though these functions are pre-set, you can also configure them as per your understanding and requirements.

· Air Frying: This function is used when you want to prepare food by using little to no oil. You can use the air frying function to crisp the cooked food or for cooking the food from the beginning. The default time set for this pre-set is 20 minutes, and the default temperature is 400°F to 204°C. And for this type of cooking, you must use the air fryer basket.

· Broiling: For broiling, you must ensure that the food is placed closer to the heating element. And you can use this function for melting food items like cheese and others. Further, the default time for broiling is set at 10 minutes, and the temperature range is similar to what we have observed in Air Frying. You can use the air frying basket or the dehydrating tray for this function.

5

· Baking: Crave some sweetness? Well, you can bake cakes, pastries, brownies, and other sweet stuff in your new attachment. And not only this, but you can also bake buns in it. For baking, the default time is 30 minutes, and the temperature is 365°F or 185°C. You must also use an appropriate utensil. Most of the time, it will be specified with the instructions of the dish you are preparing. If not, you can use an oven-safe baking dish or even an air fryer basket for this purpose.

· Roast: Lamb, pork, beef, or any other poultry item, the Instant Pot Air Fryer Lid is a great appliance that is good for all functions. Along with this, you can also enjoy roasted vegetables with the lid while using the air fryer basket for the purpose. Further, when it comes to the average time for roasting, it is 40 minutes. And the temperature settings are kept at 380°F or 193°C. The golden finish to your food comes with the smart roasting program.

· Reheating: Reheating is another smart program in the air fryer lid. It won't lead to overcooking of the food. It will only heat the food that enhances the flavour and the taste. Fifteen minutes on the clock is sufficient for reheating, and the temperature must be 280°F or 138°C.

· Dehydrating: Dehydrating takes time. That is why the average time set in the air fryer lid is 6 hours for this function. When it comes to temperature, it is best to set it at 125°F or 52°C. Dehydrating is used when you want to dry out the food items or for making fruit leather.

To play with all these functions and set the required functions, you must know the purposes of these buttons. With the Start and Cancel button, you can initiate or stop cooking. Then there are buttons to increase and decrease the time and temperature. Below them, there are six smart buttons. These intelligent functions have predetermined time and temperature, as you have read above. So, you won't have to get confused with the temperature and timings.

How Should You Use the Instant Pot Air Fryer Lid?

Well, when it comes to using the air fryer lid, there are a few prerequisites that you must follow. This includes steps like cleaning, setup, and using the right program.

Beginning from the cleaning part. It is good practice to clean the air fryer lid before using it. And after using the lid, you must wait for it to cool down and then clean it.

First Time Use:

To use the air fryer lid for the first time, you must clean it with a soft and damp cloth. This will help in removing the packaging materials from inside the lid. In no instance, you must put the lid under water or wash it with a tap. Apart from this, you can easily wash the accessories that come with the lid separately under fresh water. You can also use soap water to wash them. Afterwards, either let them dry out or use a cloth to dry them.

After this, you need to assemble the air fryer basket. Make sure to place it on a stable surface. And as per your usage requirements, you can also set the dehydrating or broiling tray inside the pot. You won't get the air fryer pot along with your purchase. However, the air frying basket, broiling and dehydrating tray, and a protective pad is included with the package.

Chapter 1:

Chicken recipes

Sweet Paprika and Rosemary Turkey

Prep time: 5 minutes

Cooking time: 30 minutes

Servings: 4

Ingredients

- 1 pound turkey breast, skinless, boneless and sliced

- 1 tablespoon olive oil

- 1 teaspoon basil, dried

- 2 cups green beans, trimmed and halved

- ½ teaspoon sweet paprika

- ½ teaspoon rosemary, dried

- ½ cup chicken stock

- A pinch of salt and black pepper

- 1 tablespoon parsley, chopped

Directions

1. Set the Air Fry mode.

2. Put turkey breast in the multi-level air fryer basket and seal the Instant Pot Duo Crisp with the air fryer lid. Brown it for 5 minutes.

3. Then add all remaining ingredients and cook the meal at 380F for 20 minutes.

Cumin Chicken

Prep time: 5 minutes

Cooking time: 25 minutes

Servings: 4

Ingredients

- 1 pound chicken breasts, skinless, boneless and halved

- 1 red bell pepper, cut into strips

- 1 green bell pepper, cut into strips

- ½ cup tomato sauce

- ½ teaspoon cumin, ground

- ½ teaspoon coriander, ground

- 2 tablespoons olive oil

- 1 tablespoon chives, chopped

Directions

1. Set the Air Fry mode.

2. Put all ingredients in the multi-level air fryer basket and seal the Instant Pot Duo Crisp with the air fryer lid.

3. Cook the meal at 380F for 25 minutes. Shake the meal in half.

Chicken Bake

Prep time: 5 minutes

Cooking time: 35 minutes

Servings: 4

Ingredients

- A pinch of salt and black pepper

- 1 cup mozzarella, shredded

- 1 pound chicken breast, skinless, boneless and cut into strips

- 1 cup red bell pepper, chopped

- 2 red onions, chopped

- ½ cup heavy cream

- 2 tablespoons butter, melted

- 1 teaspoon chili powder

- 1 garlic clove, minced

- 1 tablespoon parsley, chopped

Directions

1. Set the Air Fry mode.

2. Put chicken and onions in the multi-level air fryer basket and cook at 380F and seal the Instant Pot Duo Crisp with the air fryer lid. Cook the meal for 20 minutes.

3. Then add all remaining ingredients and cook the meal for 15 minutes more.

Chicken with Smoked Paprika

Prep time: 5 minutes

Cooking time: 20 minutes

Servings: 4

Ingredients

- 2 pounds chicken breasts, skinless, boneless and sliced

- 2 tablespoons smoked paprika

- 2 tablespoons olive oil

- 1 teaspoon chili powder

- A pinch of salt and black pepper

- 1 tablespoon cilantro, chopped

Directions

1. Set the Air Fry mode.

2. Put all ingredients in the multi-level air fryer basket, stir them gently with the help of the spatula, and seal the Instant Pot Duo Crisp with the air fryer lid.

3. Cook the meal at 350F for 10 minutes.

Tender Chicken Thighs

Prep time: 5 minutes

Cooking time: 30 minutes

Servings: 4

Ingredients

- 4 chicken thighs, boneless and skinless

- 3 tablespoons butter, melted

- Juice of 1 lime

- A pinch of salt and black pepper

- 4 garlic cloves, minced

- 1 tablespoon thyme, chopped

Directions

1. Set the Air Fry mode.

2. Put all ingredients in the multi-level air fryer basket and seal the Instant Pot Duo Crisp with the air fryer lid.

3. Cook the meal at 370F for 20 minutes.

Mojo Roast Chicken

Prep time: 4 hour

Cooking time: 50 minutes

Servings: 3

Ingredients

- 2 tsp ground cumin

- 2 tsp coarse salt

- 2 tsp dried oregano

- 2 tsp chili powder

- 1 tsp brown sugar

- 1 tsp pepper

- 1 whole chicken about 3 lbs

- 2 bay leaves

- 1 small onion quartered

- 1/4 cup orange juice

- 1/4 cup lime juice

- 1/4 cup lemon juice

- 1/4 cup olive oil divided

- 1/2 Serrano chili pepper seeded and diced

15

- 1 tbsp Dijon mustard

- 4 cloves garlic minced

- 2 cups sodium-reduced chicken broth

Directions

1. Stir together cumin, salt, oregano, chili powder, brown sugar and pepper; rub spice mixture all over and inside chicken cavity. Place chicken in large resealable plastic bag; add bay leaves and onion.

2. Whisk together orange juice, lime juice, lemon juice, 3 tbsp oil, Serrano, mustard and garlic; pour into bag. Seal bag; place bag on tray or in bowl. Refrigerate for at least 4 hours or overnight.

3. Remove chicken from marinade; reserving marinade. Place chicken breast side down in inner pot of Instant Pot Duo Crisp + Air Fryer. Add broth and reserved marinade.

4. Place lid on pot and lock into place to seal. Select Pressure Cook/Manual setting on High Pressure for 20 minutes.

5. When pressure cooking is complete, Quick Release the pressure. Once pressure is released, remove the lid.

6. Using tongs, remove chicken from inner pot; drain cooking liquid. Pat chicken dry with paper towel.

7. Ensure that inner pot is dry; place air fryer basket or trivet in pot. Drizzle remaining oil over chicken; place chicken breast side up in basket.

8. Using Air fryer Lid select Roast at 400°F for 25 minutes; continue to roast, if needed, for 5 minutes or until internal temperature of chicken reaches 165°F. Let stand for 10 minutes.

9. Slice chicken; serve with any drippings if desired.

Sweet Chicken Wings

Prep time: 5 minutes

Cooking time: 30 minutes

Servings: 4

Ingredients

- 2 pounds chicken wings, halved

- 3 tablespoons honey

- 1 tablespoon olive oil

- Juice of 1 lime

- ½ teaspoon turmeric powder

- A pinch of salt and black pepper

- 2 garlic cloves, minced

Directions

1. Set the Air Fry mode.

2. Put all ingredients in the multi-level air fryer basket and seal the Instant Pot Duo Crisp with the air fryer lid.

3. Cook the chicken wings for 30 minutes at 400F, shake the chicken wings in halfway of cooking.

Oregano and Chives Turkey

Prep time: 5 minutes

Cooking time: 30 minutes

Servings: 4

Ingredients:

- 2 pounds turkey breast, skinless, boneless and cubed

- 1 tablespoon olive oil

- 1 red onion, chopped

- 1 cup heavy cream

- Salt and black pepper to the taste

- 3 garlic cloves, minced

- ½ teaspoon oregano, dried

- ¼ cup chives, chopped

Directions

1. Set the Air Fry mode.

2. Put all ingredients in the multi-level air fryer basket and seal the Instant Pot Duo Crisp with the air fryer lid.

3. Cook the turkey for 30 minutes at 380F. Stir the meal after 15 minutes of cooking.

Orange Turkey

Prep time: 5 minutes

Cooking time: 20 minutes

Servings: 4

Ingredients

- 1 pound turkey breast, skinless, boneless and cubed

- 1 cup oranges, peeled and cut into segments

- 1 tablespoon balsamic vinegar

- 1 tablespoon olive oil

- Salt and black pepper to the taste

- 1 tablespoon orange zest, grated

Direction

1. Set the Air Fry mode.

2. Put all ingredients in the multi-level air fryer basket and seal the Instant Pot Duo Crisp with the air fryer lid.

3. Cook the turkey at 380F for 20 minutes.

4. When the meal is cooked, shake it well and transfer in the serving bowls.

Tuna and Vegetables Mix

Prep time: 5 minutes

Cooking time: 20 minutes

Servings: 4

Ingredients

- 1 pound tuna fillets, boneless and roughly cubed

- ½ cup rhubarb, sliced

- 1 cup okra, sliced

- 2 tablespoons olive oil

- 2 tablespoons balsamic vinegar

- A pinch of salt and black pepper

- 1 tablespoon parsley, chopped

Directions:

1. Set the Air Fry mode.

2. Put all ingredients in the multi-level air fryer basket and seal the Instant Pot Duo Crisp with the air fryer lid.

3. Cook the meal at 380f for 20 minutes.

Chicken, Asparagus, and Sweet Paprika

Prep time: 15 minutes

Cooking time: 25 minutes

Servings: 4

Ingredients

- 1 pound chicken breast, skinless, boneless and sliced

- ¼ pound asparagus spears, trimmed

- 1 tablespoon avocado oil

- Juice of 1 lemon

- ½ teaspoon sweet paprika

- 1 teaspoon oregano, dried

- A pinch of salt and black pepper

Directions

1. Set the Air Fry mode.

2. Put all ingredients in the multi-level air fryer basket and seal the Instant Pot Duo Crisp with the air fryer lid.

3. Cook the meal at 380F for 25 minutes.

Olives and Turkey Mix

Prep time: 10 minutes

Cooking time: 30 minutes

Servings: 4

Ingredients

- 2 pounds turkey breast, skinless, boneless and cubed

- 1 cup black olives, pitted and halved

- 1 cup tomato sauce

- 1 tablespoon avocado oil

- A pinch of salt and black pepper

- 1 teaspoon oregano, dried

- ½ teaspoon garlic powder

- ½ teaspoon sweet paprika

Directions

1. Set the Air Fry mode.

2. Put all ingredients in the multi-level air fryer basket and seal the Instant Pot Duo Crisp with the air fryer lid.

3. Cook the meal at 370F for 30 minutes.

Chicken Pockets

Prep time: 14 minutes

Cooking time: 4.5 hours

Servings: 5

Ingredients

- 4 tablespoons plain yogurt

- 1 teaspoon salt

- 1 teaspoon cilantro

- ½ teaspoon rosemary

- ½ teaspoon tomato paste

- 8 oz chicken fillet, sliced

- 1/3 cup water

- 5 pitas

- 1 sweet pepper

- 1 white onion

Directions

1. Pour water in the Instant Pot Duo Crisp Duo crisp and add the sliced chicken.

2. After this, sprinkle the meat with the salt, cilantro, and rosemary.

3. Seal Instant Pot Duo Crisp with pressure cooking lid

4. Select the Pressure Cook mode and cook on HIGH for 3 hours.

5. Meanwhile, peel the onion and cut it into the medium petals. Then discard the seeds from the sweet pepper and cut it into the strips. When the time is done, open the Instant Pot Duo Crisp lid and stir the chicken fillet gently.

6. Then add the onion petals and sweet pepper strips over the chicken fillet. Cook on HIGH for 1.5 hours more.

7. Meanwhile, make the crosswise cut in the pitas. Spread the pitas with the plain yogurt inside.

8. When the time is done, remove the chicken and vegetables from the Instant Pot Duo Crisp and chill well. Fill the pita bread with the chicken and vegetables and serve it immediately.

Jerk Chicken

Prep time: 15 minutes

Cooking time: 9 hours

Servings: 6

Ingredients

- 1 lemon

- 3-pound chicken thighs

- 1 tablespoon taco seasoning

- 1 Habaneros pepper

- 1 tablespoon garlic clove, chopped

- ¼ teaspoon ground cinnamon

- 1 teaspoon ground black pepper

- 7 oz scallions

- 1/3 teaspoon thyme

- 1 oz fresh ginger, grated

- 5 oz pineapple juice

- 2 teaspoons soy sauce

- 1 teaspoon salt

- 1/3 cup chicken stock

- 1 teaspoon butter

Directions

1. Peel the lemon and chop it. Chop Habaneros pepper. Place the chopped ingredients in the blender.

2. Add the taco seasoning, chopped garlic clove, ground cinnamon, ground black pepper, scallions, thyme, grated fresh ginger, soy sauce, salt, and butter.

3. Blend the mixture till it is smooth. After this, pour the chicken stock in the Instant Pot Duo Crisp bowl. Put the chicken thighs in the chicken stock.

4. Cover the chicken thighs with the blended spice mixture. Add the pineapple juice. Close with the pressure cooking lid and select the Pressure Cook mode, cook the dish on LOW for 9 hours.

5. When the chicken is cooked, open the lid and let it chill. Transfer the dish to the serving plates and sprinkle with the remaining sauce from the Instant Pot Duo Crisp.

Lemon and Chicken Rice

Prep time: 20 minutes

Cooking time: 9 hours

Servings: 7

Ingredients

- 16 oz chicken thighs

- 2 lemon

- 1 cup white rice

- 1 teaspoon salt

- 1 teaspoon turmeric

- 1 teaspoon ground black pepper

- 1 teaspoon cilantro

- 1 teaspoon oregano

- 1 teaspoon chili flakes

- 2 tablespoons butter

- 3 garlic cloves

- 7 oz tomatoes, canned

- 5 oz white onion

- ½ cup green peas, frozen

- 5 oz chicken stock

- 1 oz bay leaf

Directions

1. Peel the garlic cloves and slice them. Toss the butter in a sauté pan and melt it. Sprinkle the melted butter with the salt, turmeric, ground black pepper, cilantro, oregano, chili flakes, sliced garlic, and bay leaf.

2. Roast the mixture on the high heat for 30 seconds, stirring constantly. After this, place the chicken thighs in the pan and sear the chicken for 4 minutes on the both side.

3. Meanwhile, pour the chicken stock in the Instant Pot Duo Crisp bowl. Add green peas, canned tomatoes, and white rice. Peel the white onion and slice it.

4. Transfer the chicken thighs in the Instant Pot Duo Crisp. Put the sliced onion in the remaining butter mixture and roast it for 4 minutes on the medium heat. Put the roasted sliced onion in the Instant Pot Duo Crisp. Then slice the lemon and layer it in the Instant Pot Duo Crisp bowl.

5. Close with the pressure cooking lid and cook the dish on Pressure Cook mode for 9 hours on LOW. When the dish is cooked, chill it gently.

Chicken Burrito Bowl

Prep time: 20 minutes

Cooking time: 7 hours

Servings: 6

Ingredients

- 13 oz chicken breast

- 1 cup sweet corn, frozen

- 1 cup chicken stock

- 6 oz tomatoes

- 7 oz wild rice

- 5 oz red kidney beans, canned

- 1 teaspoon salt

- 1 teaspoon turmeric

- 1 teaspoon cilantro

- ½ teaspoon oregano

- 1 teaspoon chili powder

- 1 teaspoon onion powder

- 1 teaspoon garlic powder

- 1 teaspoon butter

Directions

1. Put the chicken breast in the Instant Pot Duo Crisp. Sprinkle it with the salt, turmeric, cilantro, oregano, chili powder, onion powder, and garlic powder.

2. Add chicken stock and close the lid. Cook the chicken on pressure mode (LOW pressure) for 3 hours. After this, open the lid and add sweet corn, wild rice, red kidney beans, and butter.

3. Slice the tomatoes and add them in the Instant Pot Duo Crisp as well. Close with the pressure cooking lid and cook the mixture for 4 hours on LOW more.

4. Open the Instant Pot Duo Crisp and remove the chicken breast and put in a serving bowl. Shred the chicken with the fork. Add the remaining juice from the Instant Pot Duo Crisp into the shredded chicken. Serve it!

CHICKEN CASSEROLE

Prep time: 10 minutes

Cooking time: 30 minutes

Servings: **1**

Ingredients

- 3 c chicken, shredded (I used left over rotisserie chicken)

- 12 oz bag egg noodles

- 1/2 large onion

- 1/2 c chopped carrots

- 1/4 c frozen peas

- 1/4 c frozen broccoli pieces

- 2 stalks celery chopped

- 5 c chicken broth

- 1 t garlic powder

- salt and pepper to taste

- 1 c cheddar cheese, shredded

- 1 package French's onions

- 1/4 c sour cream

- 1 can cream of chicken and mushroom soup

Directions

1. Place the chicken, vegetables, garlic powder, salt and pepper, and broth into the Instant Pot and stir.

2. Press or lightly stir the egg noodles into the mix until damp/wet.

3. Pressure cook on manual high pressure for 4 minutes.

4. Quick release.

5. Stir in the sour cream, can of soup, cheese, and 1/3 of the French's onions.

6. Top with the remaining French's onions and, using the air fry lid, air fry at 400 for 4-5 minutes until golden brown.

7. If using the oven or air fryer to crisp the top, transfer to a pan and broil or air fry until golden brown.

Chicken Tikka Kebab

Prep time: 40 minutes

Cooking time: 20 minutes

Servings: **3**

Ingredients

- 1 lb Chicken thighs boneless skinless, cut into 1.5-2 inch cubes

- 1 tbsp Oil

- ½ cup Red Onion cut into 2 inch cubes, layers separated

- ½ cup Green Bell Pepper cut into 2 inch cubes

- ½ cup Red Bell Pepper cut into 2 inch cubes

- Lime wedges to garnish

- Onion rounds to garnish

For marinade

- ½ cup Yogurt greek (also called hung curd)

- ¾ tbsp Ginger grated

- ¾ tbsp Garlic minced

- tbsp Lime juice

- tsp Kashmiri red chili powder mild, adjust to taste

- ½ tsp Ground Turmeric

- tsp Garam Masala

- 1 tsp Coriander powder

- ½ tbsp Dried Fenugreek leaves

- tsp Salt adjust to taste

Directions

1. Combine all ingredients for the marinade in a bowl and mix well. Add chicken and coat on each side with the marinade. Let it rest for anywhere between 30 minutes to 8 hours in the refrigerator.

2. When ready to cook, add the oil, onions, green and red bell pepper to the marinade. Mix well.

3. Thread the marinated chicken, peppers and onions in the skewers altenating between each.

AirFryer Method:

1. Lightly grease the air fryer basket.

2. Arrange the chicken sticks in airfryer Cook at 180 degrees or 360F for 10 minutes.

3. Turn the chicken sticks and cook for 7 more minutes, then serve

Buffalo Chicken Poutine

Prep time: 15 minutes

Cooking time: 55 minutes

Servings: **3**

Ingredients

- 2 lb potatoes cut into 1-inch wedges

- 1/4 tsp each salt and pepper

- 2 tbsp canola oil

- 1 cup shredded cooked chicken heated

- 1/2 cup shredded aged Cheddar cheese

- 1 cup cheese curds

- 1/4 cup crumbled blue cheese

- 1/3 cup Frank's Red Hot

- 1/2 cup ranch dressing divided

- 2 cups carrot and celery sticks for serving

Directions

1. Season potato wedges with salt and pepper.

2. Ensure that inner pot of Instant Pot Duo Crisp + Air Fryer is dry; place air-fryer basket in pot. In two batches, add potato wedges to basket; do not over-fill. Drizzle each batch with half of the oil.

3. Using the Air fryer Lid select Air Fry at 400°F for 22 to 24 minutes (turning basket halfway through cooking time), or until wedge fries are golden brown and cooked through.

4. Arrange potato wedges in serving dish. Top with chicken. Sprinkle with Cheddar, cheese curds and blue cheese. Drizzle with buffalo wing sauce and 2 tbsp ranch dressing. Serve with carrot and celery sticks, and remaining ranch dressing for dipping.

5. Alternatively, assemble Buffalo Chicken Poutine in small ovenproof baking dish. Place on trivet with sling in inner pot. Using the Air Fryer Lid select Broil for 2 to 3 minutes or until cheese is golden and bubbling.

Chapter 2:

Pork

Pork Satay with Peanut Sauce

Prep time: 20 minutes

cook time: 10 minutes

serves: 3-4

Ingredients

- 1 pound pork chops, cut into 1-inch cubes
- 2 garlic, minced
- 1 tablespoon fresh ginger, grated
- 2 teaspoons chili paste
- 2-3 tablespoons sweet soy sauce
- 2 tablespoons vegetable oil
- 1 shallot, finely chopped
- 1 teaspoon ground coriander
- ½ cup coconut milk
- 4 oz unsalted butter

Directions

1. Mix half of the garlic in a dish with the ginger, 1 teaspoon hot pepper sauce, 1 tablespoon soy sauce, and 1 tablespoon oil. Add the the meat to the mixture and leave to marinate for 15 minutes.

2. Preheat the air fryer to 380 F. Put the marinated meat in the air fryer basket cook for 12 minutes until brown and done. Turn once while cooking.

3. Meanwhile, make the peanut sauce. Heat 1 tablespoon of the oil in a saucepan and gently sauté the shallot with garlic. Add the coriander and cook for 1-2 minutes more.

4. Serve the meat with sauce and enjoy!

Zero Oil Pork Chops

Prep time: 5 minutes

cook time: 15 minutes

serves: 2

Ingredients

- 2 pieces pork chops
- 1 tablespoon of plain flour
- 1 large egg
- 2 tablespoon breadcrumbs
- Salt and black pepper to taste

Directions

1. First, you need to preheat the air fryer to 360 F.

2. Then, season pork chops with salt and black pepper and set aside.

3. Beat the egg in the plate. In another plate place the flour and in the third plate breadcrumbs.

4. Cover each pork chop with the flour on both sides, then, dip in the egg, then, cover with breadcrumbs. Make sure that meat covered from all sides.

5. Place pork chops in the air fryer and cook for 15 minutes, until they are tender and crispy. Turn once while cooking, to cook the meat from both sides.

6. Serve with fresh vegetables or mashed potatoes.

Drunken Ham with Mustard

Prep time: 10 minutes

cook time: 40 minutes

serves: 4

Ingredients

- 1 joint of ham, approximately 1-2 pounds
- 2 tablespoon honey
- 2 tablespoon French mustard
- 8 oz whiskey
- 1 teaspoon Provencal herbs
- 1 tablespoon salt

Directions

1. In a large casserole dish that fits in your Air Fryer prepare the marinade: combine the whiskey, honey and mustard.

2. Place the ham in the oven dish and turn it in the marinade.

3. Preheat the Air Fryer to 380 F and cook the ham for 15 minutes.

4. Serve with potatoes and fresh vegetables.

Easy Steak Sticks

Prep time: 5 minutes

cook time: 20 minutes

serves: 3

Ingredients

- 1 pound steak
- 2 tablespoon olive oil
- 1 teaspoon dried thyme
- 1 teaspoon dried parsley
- A pinch of chili powder
- Salt and pepper to taste
- Sesame seeds for garnish

Directions

1. Cut the steak into 1-inch strips.

2. In the mixing bowl combine the olive oil and dried herbs. Add chili powder and stir to combine.

3. Preheat the air fryer to 370 F.

4. Lay meat strips to the working surface. Evenly season meat with salt and black pepper. Skewer the steak strips to the skewers. Dip the meat in the oil mixture and place to the air fryer basket. Cook for 15-20 minutes, until brown and crispy.

5. Serve with cooked rice or mashed potatoes. You can also garnish the meat with sesame seeds and freshly chopped herbs of your choice.

Delicate Steak with Garlic

Prep time: 10 minutes

cook time: 30 minutes

serves: 3

Ingredients

- 1 pound halibut steak
- 2/3 cup soy sauce
- ¼ cup sugar
- ½ cup Japanese cooking wine
- 2 tablespoons lime juice
- 1 garlic clove, crushed
- ¼ cup orange juice
- ¼ teaspoon ground ginger
- ¼ teaspoon crushed red pepper flakes
- ½ teaspoon salt

Directions

1. All ingredients mix in a saucepan and make a fine marinade

2. Bring to a boil over high heat. Divide in halves.

3. One half of the marinade put with the halibut in releasable bag and set aside in the refrigerator for 30 minutes.

4. Preheat the air fryer to 390°F and cook marinated steak for 10-12 minutes.

5. The other half of the marinade serves with cooked steak.

Pork Loin with Potatoes and Herbs

Prep time: 10 minutes

cook time: 30 minutes

serves: 4

Ingredients

- 2-pound pork loin
- 2 large potatoes, large dice
- ½ teaspoon garlic powder
- ½ teaspoon red pepper flakes
- 1 teaspoon dried parsley, crushed
- ½ teaspoon black pepper, freshly ground
- A pinch of salt
- Balsamic glaze to taste

Directions

1. Sprinkle the pork loin with garlic powder, red pepper flakes, parsley, salt, and pepper.

2. Preheat the air fryer to 370 F and place the pork loin, then the potatoes next to the pork in the basket of the air fryer and close. Cook for about 20-25 minutes.

3. Remove the pork loin from the air fryer. Let it rest for a few minutes before slicing.

4. Place the roasted potatoes to the serving plate. Slice the pork. Place 4-5 slices over the potatoes and drizzle the balsamic glaze over the pork.

Pork Chops Fried

Prep time: 20 minutes

cook time: 25 minutes

serves: 3

Ingredients

- 3-4 pieces pork chops (cut in 1-inch thick, roughly 10 oz each)
- ¼ cup olive oil, divided
- 1 tablespoon cilantro, chopped
- 1 tablespoon parsley, chopped
- 1 tablespoon rosemary, chopped
- 1 tablespoon Dijon mustard
- 1 tablespoon coriander, ground
- 1-2 teaspoon salt to taste
- 1 teaspoon sugar

Directions

1. In the large mixing bowl combine 1/4 cup olive oil, 1 tablespoon cilantro, parsley, rosemary, Dijon mustard, coriander. Add some salt and black pepper. Dip the meat to the mixture, then transfer to a re-sealable bag and refrigerate for 2-3 hours.

2. Preheat the Air Fryer to 390°F.

3. Remove the pork chops out of the refrigerator and let sit at room temp for 30 minutes prior to cooking.

4. Reheat the Air Fryer to 390°F.

5. Cook 1 to 2 pork chops in the Air Fryer for 10-12 minutes. Please note: thinner cuts will cook faster. Take 2 minutes off the cooking time for thinner cuts.

6. Serve with mashed potatoes or other garnish you prefer.

Chinese Roast Pork

Prep time: 5 minutes

cook time: 25 minutes

serves: 4

Ingredients

- 2 pounds of pork shoulder
- 2 tablespoons sugar
- 1 tablespoon honey
- 1/3 cup of soy sauce
- 1/2 tablespoon salt

Directions

1. Cut the meat in large pieces. Place to a large bowl and add all ingredients to make a marinade. Stir to combine well to coat all the meat pieces.

2. Preheat the air fryer to 350 F. Transfer marinated meat and cook for about 10 minutes, stirring couple times while cooking.

3. Increase the temperature to 400 F and cook for another 3-5 minutes until completely cooked

Mouth Watering Pork Tenderloin with Bell Pepper

Prep time: 7 minutes

cook time: 15 minutes

serves: 3

Ingredients

- 1 pound pork tenderloin
- 2 medium-sized yellow or red bell peppers, cut into strips
- 1 little onion, sliced
- 2 teaspoons Provencal herbs
- Salt and black pepper to taste
- 1 tablespoon olive oil

Directions

1. In the large mixing bowl combine sliced bell peppers, onions, and Provencal herbs. Season with salt and pepper to taste. Sprinkle with the olive oil and set aside.

2. Cut the pork tenderloin into 1-inch cubes and rub with salt and black pepper.

3. Preheat the air fryer to 370 F.

4. On the bottom of the air fryer basket lay seasoned meat and coat with vegetable mixture. Fry for 15 minutes, turning the meat and veggies once while cooking.

5. Serve with mashed potatoes.

Cheesy Pork Fillets

Prep time: 8 minutes

cook time: 20 minutes

serves: 3

Ingredients

- 3 pork filets
- 2 large eggs, beaten
- 1 cup all-purpose flour
- 3 slices swiss cheese
- Salt and black pepper to taste

Directions

1. Preheat the air fryer to 380 F.

2. Dip pork fillets in egg and top each fillet with cheese slice. Season with salt and pepper and cover each piece with little more egg and then coat in all-purpose flour.

3. Place these "patties" in the air fryer and cook for 20 minutes, turning once during cooking.

4. When ready, serve hot and enjoy!

Chapter 3

Beef recipes

Steak Tips with Potatoes

Preparation Time: 10 minutes Cooking Time: 20 minutes Serving: 2

Ingredients

- 1/2 lb steak, cut into 1/2-inch cubes

- 1/4 lb potatoes, cut into 1/2-inch cubes

- 1/4 tsp garlic powder

- 1/2 tsp Worcestershire sauce

- 1 tbsp butter, melted

- Pepper

- Salt

Directions

1. Cook potatoes into the boiling water for 5 minutes. Drain well and set aside.

2. In a mixing bowl, toss together steak cubes, potatoes, garlic powder, Worcestershire sauce, butter, pepper, and salt.

3. Spray instant pot multi-level air fryer basket with cooking spray.

4. Add steak potato mixture into the air fryer basket and place basket into the instant pot.

5. Seal pot with air fryer lid and select air fry mode then set the temperature to 400 F and timer for 20 minutes. mix halfway through.

6. Serve and enjoy.

Nutrition

- Calories 318

- Fat 11.5 g

- Carbohydrates 9.4 g

- Sugar 1 g

- Protein 42 g

- Cholesterol 117 mg

Asian Beef Broccoli

Preparation Time: 10 minutes Cooking Time: 15 minutes Serving: 3

Ingredients

- 1/2 lb steak, cut into strips

- 1 tsp garlic, minced

- 1 tsp ginger, minced

- 2 tbsp sesame oil

- 2 tbsp soy sauce

- 1/3 cup oyster sauce

- 1 lb broccoli florets

Directions

1. Add steak into the mixing bowl. Add remaining ingredients and mix well and set aside for 1 hour.

2. Spray instant pot multi-level air fryer basket with cooking spray.

3. Add marinated steak pieces and broccoli into the air fryer basket and place basket into the instant pot.

4. Seal pot with air fryer lid and select air fry mode then set the temperature to 350 F and timer for 15 minutes. mix halfway through.

5. Serve and enjoy.

Nutrition

- Calories 295

- Fat 13.4 g

- Carbohydrates 12.4 g

- Sugar 2.8 g

- Protein 32.4 g

- Cholesterol   68   mg

Simple Steak

Preparation time: 6minutes Cooking time: 14 minutes Servings: 2

Ingredients:

- ½ pound quality cuts steak

- Salt and freshly ground black pepper, to taste

- Directions:

- Preparing the ingredients. Preheat the instant crisp air fryer to 390 degrees f.

- Rub the steak with salt and pepper evenly.

- Air frying. Place the steak in the instant crisp air fryer basket, close air fryer lid and cook for about 14 minutes crispy.

Lamb Loin and Tomato Vinaigrette

Preparation time: 40 minutes Cooking time: 10 minutes Servings: 4

Ingredients:

- 4 lamb loin slices

- 3 garlic cloves; minced

- 1/3 cup parsley; chopped

- 1/3 cup sun-dried tomatoes; chopped

- 2 tbsp. Balsamic vinegar

- 2 tbsp. Water

- 2 tbsp. Olive oil

- 2 tsp. Thyme; chopped

- A pinch of salt and black pepper

Directions:

1. In a blender, combine all the ingredients except the lamb slices and pulse well.

2. Take a bowl and mix the lamb with the tomato vinaigrette and toss well

3. Put the lamb in your air fryer's basket and cook at 380°f for 15 minutes on each side

4. Divide everything between plates and serve.

Nutrition: Calories: 273; Fat: 13g; Fiber: 4g; Carbs: 6g; Protein: 17g

Beef Taco Fried Egg Rolls

Preparation time: 10 minutes Cooking time: 12 minutes Servings: 8

Ingredients

- 1 tsp. Cilantro

- 2 chopped garlic cloves

- 1 tbsp. Olive oil

- 1 c. Shredded Mexican cheese

- ½ packet taco seasoning

- ½ can cilantro lime rotel

- ½ chopped onion

- 16 egg roll wrappers

- 1-pound lean ground beef

Directions:

1. Preparing the ingredients. Ensure that your instant crisp air fryer is preheated to 400 degrees.

2. Add onions and garlic to a skillet, cooking till fragrant. Then add taco seasoning, pepper, salt, and beef, cooking till beef is broke up into tiny pieces and cooked thoroughly.

3. Add rotel and stir well.

4. Lay out egg wrappers and brush with water to soften a bit.

5. Load wrappers with beef filling and add cheese to each.

6. Fold diagonally to close and use water to secure edges.

7. Brush filled egg wrappers with olive oil and add to the instant crisp air fryer.

8. Air frying. Close air fryer lid. Set temperature to 400°f, and set time to 8 minutes. Cook 8 minutes, flip, and cook another 4 minutes.

9. Served sprinkled with cilantro.

Nutrition: Calories: 348; Fat: 11g; Protein:24g; Sugar:1g

Air Fryer Meatloaf

Preparation: 10 minutes Cooking time: 25 minutes Servings: 4

Ingredients:

- 1-pound lean beef

- 1 egg, medium, lightly beaten

- 3 tablespoons breadcrumbs

- 1 onion, small, finely chopped

- 1 tablespoon fresh thyme, chopped

- 1 teaspoon kosher salt

- ½ teaspoon ground black pepper

- 2 mushrooms, medium, sliced

- 1 tablespoon olive oil

Directions:

1. Wash beef and pat dry.

2. In a medium-large bowl, combine beef, egg, breadcrumbs, salt, thyme, onion, and pepper. Knead and mix the ingredients well.

3. Transfer this mix into a baking pan and place the mushroom on top of the mix.

4. Coat this mix with olive oil and place the pan in the air fryer basket.

5. Now put the air fryer basket in the inner pot of instant pot air fryer.

6. Close the crisp cover.

7. Under the roast mode, set the timer for 25 minutes and let the meatloaf roast. The smart roast option will automatically select the temperature to 380°f.

8. Press the start button to resume the cooking.

9. After cooking, allow the meatloaf to settle down the heat before you can slice and serve it.

10. Slice it into small portions and serve.

Nutrition: Calories 297, carbohydrates: 5.9g, fat 18.8g, protein: 24.8g, cholesterol 126mg, sodium:706mg, sugars: 1g. Saturate fat: 6g, potassium: 361mg, calcium: 33mg

Baked Carrot Beef

Preparation time:5-10 Minutes

Cooking Time: 60 Minutes

Serving: 5-6

Ingredients:

- 2 carrots, chopped

- 2 sticks celery, chopped

- 3 pounds beef

- Olive oil to taste

- 2 medium onions, sliced

- Garlic cloves from 1 bunch

- 1 bunch mixed fresh herbs (thyme, rosemary, bay, sage etc.) Directions:

- Grease a baking pan with some cooking spray. Add the vegetables, beef roast, olive oil, and herbs; combine well.

- Place Instant Pot Air Fryer Crisp over kitchen platform. Press Air Fry, set the temperature to 400°F and set the timer to 5 minutes to preheat. Press "Start" and allow it to preheat for 5 minutes.

- In the inner pot, place the Air Fryer basket. In the basket, add the pan.

- Close the Crisp Lid and press the "Bake" setting. Set temperature to 380°F and set the timer to 60 minutes. Press "Start."

- Open the Crisp Lid after cooking time is over. Serve warm.

Nutrition:

- Calories: 306

- Fat: 21g

- Saturated Fat: 7g

- Trans Fat: 0g

- Carbohydrates: 10g

- Fiber: 3g

- Sodium: 324mg

- Protein: 32g

Smoky Steak

Preparation Time: 10 minutes Cooking Time: 5 minutes Serving: 2

Ingredients:

- 12 oz steaks
- 1 tsp liquid smoke
- 1 tbsp soy sauce
- 1/2 tbsp cocoa powder
- 1 tbsp Montreal steak seasoning
- Pepper
- Salt

Directions:

1. Add steak, liquid smoke, and soy sauce in a zip-lock bag and shake well.
2. Season steak with seasonings and place in the refrigerator overnight.
3. Place the dehydrating tray in a multi-level air fryer basket and place basket in the instant pot.
4. Place marinated steak on dehydrating tray.
5. Seal pot with air fryer lid and select air fry mode then set the temperature to 375 F and timer for 5 minutes.
6. Serve and enjoy.

Nutrition:

- Calories 356

- Fat 8.7 g

- Carbohydrates 1.4 g

- Sugar 0.2 g

- Protein 62.2 g

- Cholesterol 153 mg

Herb Garlic Lamb Chops

Preparation Time: 10 minutes Cooking Time: 6 minutes Serving: 3

Ingredients:

- 3 lamb loin chops
- 1 tbsp lemon juice
- 1 tbsp lemon zest, grated
- 2 tsp dried rosemary
- 1 tsp dried thyme
- 1 tbsp olive oil
- 2 tsp garlic, minced

Directions:

1. Mix together lemon juice, lemon zest, rosemary, thyme, oil, and garlic and rub over lamb chops.
2. Place the dehydrating tray in a multi-level air fryer basket and place basket in the instant pot.
3. Place lamb chops on dehydrating tray.
4. Seal pot with air fryer lid and select air fry mode then set the temperature to 400 F and timer for 6 minutes. Turn lamb chops halfway through.
5. Serve and enjoy.

Nutrition:

- Calories 300

- Fat 14.8 g

- Carbohydrates 1.9 g

- Sugar 0.3 g

- Protein 38.2 g

- Cholesterol 122 mg

Delicious Lamb Chops

Preparation Time: 10 minutes Cooking Time: 8 minutes Serving: 4

Ingredients:

- 1 lb lamb chops

- 2 tbsp lemon juice

- 2 tbsp olive oil

- 1 tsp ground coriander

- 1 tsp oregano

- 1 tsp thyme

- 1 tsp rosemary

- 1 tsp salt

Directions:

1. Add lamb chops and remaining ingredients into the zip-lock bag. Shake well and place it in the refrigerator for 1 hour.

2. Place the dehydrating tray in a multi-level air fryer basket and place basket in the instant pot.

3. Place lamb chops on dehydrating tray.

4. Seal pot with air fryer lid and select air fry mode then set the temperature to 400 F and timer for 8 minutes. Turn lamb chops halfway through.

5. Serve and enjoy.

Nutrition:

- Calories 276

- Fat 15.5 g

- Carbohydrates 0.8 g

- Sugar 0.2 g

- Protein 32 g

Garlic Roasted Pork Tenderloin

Preparation time:5-10 Minutes

Cooking Time: 18 Minutes

Serving: 5-6

Ingredients:

- ¼ teaspoon ground black pepper

- ¼ teaspoon garlic powder

- ¼ teaspoon salt

- 1 ½ pound pork tenderloin

- 1 tablespoon olive oil

Directions:

1. In a mixing bowl, add the olive oil, black pepper, salt, and garlic powder. Combine the ingredients to mix well with each other. Rub the mixture evenly over the pork tenderloin.

2. Place Instant Pot Air Fryer Crisp over kitchen platform. Press Air Fry, set the temperature to 400°F and set the timer to 5 minutes to preheat. Press "Start" and allow it to preheat for 5 minutes.

3. In the inner pot, place the Air Fryer basket. In the basket, add the tenderloins.

4. Close the Crisp Lid and press the "Roast" setting. Set temperature to 400°F and set the timer to 25 minutes. Press "Start."

5. Halfway down, open the Crisp Lid, flip the tenderloin and close the lid to continue cooking for the remaining time.

6. Open the Crisp Lid after cooking time is over. Slice and serve warm.

Nutrition:

- Calories: 203

- Fat: 6g

- Saturated Fat: 1.5g

- Trans Fat: 0g

- Carbohydrates: 2g

- Fiber: 0g

- Sodium: 173mg

Crispy Breaded Pork Chops in the Air Fryer

Preparation: 10 minutes Cooking: 12 minutes Servings: 6

Ingredients:

- 6 pork chops, center cut, boneless

- 1 egg, large, beaten

- ½ cup panko breadcrumbs

- ⅓ cup corn flakes crumbs, crushed

- 2 tablespoons parmesan cheese, grated

- 1¼ teaspoon sweet paprika

- 1½ teaspoon garlic powder

- ¼ teaspoon chili powder

- ½ teaspoon onion powder

- ½ teaspoon ground black pepper

- 1 teaspoon kosher salt

- Olive oil cooking spray

Directions:

1. Cut and remove excess fat of the pork.

2. Wash and pat dry.

71

3. Spray the air fryer basket with cooking oil and place it in the inner pot of the Instant Pot Air Fryer.

4. Close the crisp cover.

5. Set the air fryer temperature to 400°F and preheat for 5 minutes in the AIR FRY mode.

6. Press START to begin the preheating.

7. In the meantime, season the pork chops by rubbing half teaspoon salt on both sides and keep aside.

8. In a large shallow bowl, combine panko breadcrumbs, cornflakes, cheese, salt, garlic powder, paprika, chili powder, onion powder, and pepper.

9. In a medium shallow bowl, beat the egg.

10. Now batch by batch, do the breading and seasoning.

11. First, dip the pork chops in the beaten egg and then dredge in the breadcrumbs mix and press it gently so that it will have good breadcrumb coating on all sides.

12. Once the preheat timer goes off, put the pork chops in the air fryer basket in batches and spritz some more cooking oil.

13. Close the crisp cover.

14. In the AIR FRY mode, at 400°F, select the timer for 40 minutes.

15. Press START to begin the cooking.

16. Halfway through the cooking, open the air fryer, and flip the pork chop.

17. To complete the remaining portion of the cooking, close the crisp cover. The Instant Pot will automatically resume cooking, from the point you have interrupted.

18. Once done, keep it aside and repeat the process with the rest of the batch.

Easy Air Fryer Pork Chops

Preparation: 10 minutesCooking: 20 minutesServings: 4

Ingredients:

- 5 ounces (4 pieces) pork chops, center-cut
- ½ cup parmesan cheese, grated
- 1 teaspoon parsley, dried
- 1 teaspoon ground paprika
- ½ teaspoon ground black pepper
- 1 teaspoon garlic powder
- 1 teaspoon salt
- 2 tablespoon olive oil, extra-virgin
- Olive cooking oil spray

Directions:

1. Wash pork chops and pat dry.
2. In a large bowl, combine the parmesan cheese, pepper, parsley, salt, garlic powder, and paprika.
3. Coat the pork chops with the olive oil and then dredge them in the parmesan mixture one by one and place it on a plate.
4. Spritz cooking oil in the air fryer basket and place in the inner pot of the Instant Pot Air Fryer.
5. Place these chops in the air fryer basket in batches.

6. Close the crisp lid.

7. Under the ROAST mode, select the timer for 25 minutes. The temperature by default will remain at 400°F.

8. Press START to begin the cooking.

9. Flip it halfway through for even cooking.

10. Once the cooking over, transfer the pork chop on a cutting board and let it rest for about 5 minutes before you slice and serve.

Chapter 4

Lamb recipes

Italian-style Air-fried Meatballs

Preparation Time: 25 minutes

Cooking Time: 15 minutes

Yields: 12 servings

Ingredients

- 1 medium-size shallot, minced
- 2 tbsps. olive oil
- 2 tbsps. whole milk
- 2 onions, chopped
- 3 cloves garlic, minced
- 2/3 lb. lean ground beef
- 1 large egg, lightly beaten
- ⅓ lb. bulk turkey sausage
- ¼ cup fresh flat-leaf parsley, finely chopped
- 1 tbsp. Dijon mustard
- 1 tbsp. fresh thyme, finely chopped
- 1 tbsp. fresh rosemary, finely chopped
- ½ tsp. Kosher salt
- 1 cup panko bread crumbs

Directions

1. Sauté garlic and onions in the Instant Pot using and cover with the Pressure cooker lid. Set to Sauté function and cook for 1-2 minutes. Remove garlic and shallot from the pot.
2. Combine panko bread crumbs and milk in a large bowl and let them stand for about 5 minutes.

3. Mix the shallot and garlic to the breadcrumb mixture together with the turkey sausage, beef, and the rest of the remaining ingredients.

4. Gently shape the batter into 1½-inch balls using your hands. Place meatballs in the air fryer basket lined with parchment paper over a raised trivet inside the Instant Pot. Cook in batches to avoid overcrowding. Cover the instant pot using the air fryer lid this time and set cooking to 400 degrees F for 10-11 minutes. Remove from the basket to cook the remaining meatballs using the same process.

Air Fryer Lamb Chops

Preparation Time: **5 minutes**

Cook Time: 15 minutes

Yields: 3 servings

Ingredients

- 3 (6 oz) pork chops
- 2 tsps. olive oil
- Salt and black pepper to taste
- A dash of paprika

Directions

1. Cleanse pork chops and pat dry. Put in a large mixing bowl and add the olive oil. Add salt and pepper to taste along with paprika and combine to allow the flavor to seep through the pork chops. Leave for a while to marinate.

2. Place the air fryer basket in the instant pot and arrange pork chops inside. You don't need to cook in batches as instant pot duo crisp has a two-layered basket to accommodate your recipe in one sitting. Attach the air fryer lid and set to 380 degrees F and cook for 10-14 minutes, flipping pork chops halfway through cooking.

3. Test for tenderness and cook more if you want it to be crispier.

4. Serve warm.

Air Fryer Bacon Recipe

Cooking Time: 10 minutes

Yields: **4 servings**

Ingredients

- 8 slices of bacon

Directions

1. Arrange bacon slices in a single layer in the instant pot duo crisp air fryer basket.
2. Attach the air fryer lid and set to air frying.
3. Cook at 400 degrees F for 8-10 minutes, flipping halfway through.
4. Serve while crispy.

Air Fryer Steak Bites & Mushrooms

Preparation Time: **10 minutes**

Cooking Time: **20 minutes**

Yields: 4 servings

Ingredients

- 8 oz. mushrooms, cleaned, washed and halved
- 1 lb. steaks, cut into 1-inch cubes and patted dry
- 2 tbsps. butter, melted
- ½ tsp. garlic powder
- 1 tsp. Worcestershire sauce
- A dash of minced parsley for garnish
- Optional: melted butter or chili flakes for finishing
- Black pepper and salt to taste

Directions

1. Add steak cubes and mushrooms in a bowl and coat with melted butter. Season the dish with garlic powder, Worcestershire sauce, salt and pepper to taste.
2. Arrange mushrooms and steak cubes in the instant pot air fryer basket. Set to air fry at 400 degrees F for 10-18 minutes, flipping from time to time for even cooking.
3. If you desire your steaks to be crispier, cook for an additional 2-5 minutes.
4. Garnish with parsley and drizzle with melted butter or chili flakes if desired. Adjust seasoning with salt and pepper if needed.
5. Serve warm.

Air Fryer Steak Tips

Preparation Time: **10 minutes**

Cooking Time: **20 minutes**

Yields: 4 servings

Ingredients

- ½ lb. potatoes, peeled and cut into half-inch pieces
- 1 lb. steaks, cut into half-inch cubes and pat dry
- 2 tbsps. melted butter, oil for alternative
- 1 tsp. Worcestershire sauce
- ½ tsp. garlic powder
- Salt and black pepper to taste
- A pinch of minced parsley for garnish
- Optional: melted butter or chili flakes for finishing

Directions

1. Add potatoes to the instant pot duo crisp and boil for about 5 minutes or until tender, using the pressure cooker lid. Drain and set aside.
2. In a mixing bowl, toss together potatoes and steak cubes with melted butter, garlic powder, and Worcestershire sauce. Season with salt and pepper to taste.
3. Spread steak cubes and potatoes in the air fryer basket. Using the air fryer lid, air-fry at 400 degrees F for 10-18 minutes, shaking and flipping potatoes halfway through cooking, depending on preferred crispness. If you want your steak cubes to be more crispy, cook for another 2-5 minutes.
4. Garnish with parsley, and drizzle with melted butter if desired. You may also use chili flakes.
5. Serve warm.

Spicy Korean Lamb Chops

Preparation Time: **20 minutes**

Cooking Time: **65 minutes**

Yields: 5 servings

Ingredients

- 2 lbs Lamb chops

For the sauce

- 6 1/2 tsp Red pepper powder

- 2 tbsp granulated sugar

- 1 tbsp curry powder

- 8 1/2 tbsp soy sauce

- 3 tbsp rice wine

- 2` tbsp garlic

- 1 tsp Ginger

- 2 tbsp Korean red pepper paste

- 2 tbsp ketchup

- 6 tbsp Corn syrup

- 1/2 tbsp sesame oil

- 1/2 tsp cinnamon powder

- 1 tsp sesame seeds

- 1 tsp black pepper

- 1/3 cup Asian pear **ground**

- 1/3 cup onion powder

- 1/2 tbsp Green plum extract

- 2 cups Water

- 1 cup red wine

- 3 bay leaves

- 1 cup carrots

- 2 cups onions

- 1 cup celery

To serve with:

- cilantro

- green onions

Directions

1. Place all the ingredients (except cilantro and green onions) into the Instant Pot inner pot and close and seal the lid. (Note: Do not cut or separate the lamb chops, cook the whole rack as one unit.)

2. Select the **Pressure Cook/Manual** button and set the time for **20 minutes** on **High** pressure.

3. Natural release for 10-15 min, then open the stem release valve to release the rest of the pressure. Remove the lamb set it aside to cool.

4. **To thicken sauce**. Press **Cancel** then select **Sauté** and toggle to **High**. Stir constantly as the sauce cooks to prevent burning. Press **Cancel** once it has thickened.

5. Pour the sauce into a bowl and clean the inner pot.

6. Cut the lamb chops away from the rack by slicing between the bones. If using a Duo Crisp, arrange lamb chops individually in a single layer on the dehydration rack and place into the air fry basket. Put the air fry basket into the cooker pot. If using a regular Instant Pot with the Air Fryer Lid, put the chops on a trivet in the inner pot. Brush additional sauce over the lamb chops.

7. Put the air fryer lid onto the Instant Pot. **Broil** at 400°F for **5 minutes**. Once they are nicely charred, remove lamp chops and set aside. Repeat the process until all of the lamb chops have been broiled.

8. Serve with chopped cilantro and green onions. (Optional)

Air-fried Garlic-rosemary Lamb Chops

Preparation Time: **3 minutes**

Cooking Time: **12 minutes**

Yields: 2 servings

Ingredients

- 2 lamb chops
- 1 clove of garlic
- 2 tsps. olive oil
- 2 tsps. garlic puree
- A sprig of fresh rosemary
- Salt and pepper to taste

Directions

1. Place lamb chops in a bowl and season with salt and pepper and brush or spray with olive oil.
2. Top each lamb chop with garlic puree.
3. Between each chops place fresh rosemary and unpeeled garlic.
4. Leave the bowl with the lamb chops in the refrigerator for about an hour to marinate.
5. Transfer the marinated lamb chops to the instant pot duo crisp air fryer basket and air-fry at 360 degrees F for 6 minutes.
6. Flip lamb chops for even cooking and cook for another 6 minutes without changing the cooking temperature.
7. Leave to rest for a minute or 2.
8. Discard the fresh garlic and rosemary and serve.

Air Fryer Sweet and Sour

Preparation Time: **15 minutes**

Cooking Time: **12 minutes**

Yields: 4 servings

Ingredients

- 2 lbs. pork, cut into chunks
- 1 cup potato starch
- 3 tbsps. canola oil
- 2 large eggs
- ¼ tsp. Chinese Five Spice
- Sea salt to taste
- 1 tsp. sesame oil, optional
- For Sweet and Sour
- ½ tsp. garlic powder
- 1 tbsp. ketchup
- ½ cup white sugar
- 1 tbsp. low-sodium soy sauce
- ½ cup seasoned rice vinegar

Directions

For Sweet and Sour Sauce

1. To make the sweet and sour sauce, add all sweet and sour sauce ingredients into the instant pot duo and cover with the pressure cooker lid. Set to Sauté mode and cook for about 5 minutes. Transfer to a bowl and reserve for later use.

Combine all seasonings in a mixing bowl (pepper, Chinese Five Spice and potato starch).

1. Add beaten eggs and sesame oil in a separate bowl.

2. Dredge pork pieces in the potato starch, shaking off any excess starch. Dip one by one into the egg mixture, again shaking to drip off before dipping back to the potato starch mix.

3. Grease instant pot air fryer basket with oil and arrange pork pieces inside. Spray oil on top and attach the air fryer lid for cover.

4. Set to air fry and cook at 340 degrees F for 8-12 minutes until cooked, shaking air fryer basket halfway through cooking.

5. Serve with Sweet and Sour Sauce.

Baby Back Ribs

Preparation Time: **15 minutes**

Cooking Time: **35 minutes**

Yields: 4 servings

Ingredients

- 1 tbsp. olive oil
- 1 rack baby back ribs
- 1 tbsp. liquid smoke flavoring
- 1 tbsp. brown sugar
- ½ tsp. garlic powder
- ½ tsp. chili powder
- 1 cup BBQ sauce
- ½ tsp. ground black pepper
- ½ tsp. onion powder
- ½ tsp. salt

Directions

1. Cleanse ribs by removing membranes on the back part and run through tap water. Pat dry with a paper towel. Cut ribs into 4 portions.
2. In a mixing bowl, combine liquid smoke with oil and rub ribs on both sides.
3. Add pepper, brown sugar, garlic powder, onion powder, chili powder in a mixing bowl. Also, add salt and pepper. Mix well to combine and rub or brush both sides of the ribs with the seasoning mix. Set aside for 30 minutes to absorb.

4. Place ribs with bone-side down in the air fryer basket. Place the basket back to the instant pot duo crisp and cover with the air fryer lid. Set to cook for 15 minutes at 375 degrees F. Flip over and cook for another 10 minutes.

5. Remove basket from the air fryer and brush ribs with the BBQ sauce.

6. Return the air fryer basket to the instant pot and cook for another 5 minutes or until desired crispness is achieved.

Meatballs

Preparation Time: **10 minutes**

Cooking Time: **10 minutes**

Yields: 12 servings

Ingredients

- 8 oz. ground Italian sausage, mild or hot
- 1 large egg
- ½ cup panko bread crumbs
- 12 oz. ground pork
- ½ tsp. dried paprika
- 1 tsp. dried parsley
- 1 tsp. salt

Directions

1. In a large bowl, combine bread crumbs, sausage, pork, egg, paprika, and parsley. Season with salt. Mix to thoroughly combine all ingredients.

2. Form into 12 meatballs of equal sizes, using an ice cream scoop. Place meatballs in an air fryer basket lined with parchment paper. You may use a two-layer of air fryer basket to accommodate all meatballs in a single batch.

3. Place the air fryer basket in the instant pot duo crisp and attach the air fryer lid. Set to 350 degrees F and cook for 8 minutes. Shake basket and cook for another 2 minutes. Transfer to a platter and serve.

Chapter 5

Vegetarian recipes

Crispy Brussels Sprouts

Preparation Time: **5 minutes**

Cooking Time: **16 minutes**

Yields: 2 servings

Ingredients

- 2 tbsps. Parmesan, freshly grated
- ½ lb. Brussels sprouts, thinly sliced
- 1 tsp. garlic powder
- 1 tbsp. extra-virgin olive oil
- Caesar dressing for dipping
- Freshly ground black pepper to taste
- Kosher salt to taste

Directions

1. Add oil, Brussels sprouts, garlic powder and Parmesan in a large mixing bowl. Toss to combine thoroughly. Season with salt and pepper.
2. Put the coated sprouts in the air fryer basket.
3. Garnish with Parmesan. You can serve with Caesar salad for a dip.

Roasted Asparagus

Prep Time: 4 minutes

Cook Time: 10 minutes

Yields: 4 servings

Ingredients

- 1 lb. asparagus with ends trimmed and cut into pieces
- 1-2 tsps. olive oil
- Salt and black pepper to taste

Directions

1. Place the asparagus pieces in a shallow dish and coat them with olive oil. Season with salt and pepper. Make sure to properly coat the asparagus ends to prevent them from burning or drying out quickly.

2. Place asparagus inside the air fryer basket and put inside the instant pot duo crisp. Choose the air fryer lift for cover, secure, and set to air frying at 380 degrees F for 7-10 minutes. Shake basket halfway through cooking to cook asparagus evenly.

3. Taste for seasoning and tenderness. Adjust if needed.

4. Serve warm.

Air Fryer Crispy Broccoli

Preparation Time: **5 minutes**

Cooking Time: **15 minutes**

Yields: 4 servings

Ingredients

- 2 tbsps. cooking oil
- 1 lb. broccoli, cut into bite-sized pieces
- ½ tsp. garlic powder
- Salt and pepper to taste
- 2 fresh lemon wedges

Directions

1. Add broccoli to a large bowl and drizzle evenly with olive oil.
2. Put in the instant pot duo crisp air fryer basket and cover with the air fryer lid.
3. Air Fry at 380 degrees F for 12-15 minutes, flipping and shaking 3 times through cooking and cook until crispy.
4. Serve with lemon wedges.

Air Fried Acorn Squash

Preparation Time: **15 minutes**

Cooking Time: **20 minutes**

Yields: 4 servings

Ingredients

- 1 acorn squash
- 3 tbsps. butter, melted
- 2 tsps. brown sugar
- ½ tsp. Kosher salt
- Black pepper to taste
- Optional toppings: melted butter, roasted nuts (chopped), pomegranate seeds

Direction

1. Cleanse the squash and trim the ends. Cut in half and core to remove seeds. Cut into about half an inch thick.
2. Combine brown sugar and melted butter in a bowl. Season with salt and pepper.
3. Add in the acorn squash and toss to coat.
4. Place the coated squash into the air fryer basket and attach the air fryer lid to the instant pot. Set to air fry at 375 degrees F for 15-20 minutes or until tender, flipping after 10 minutes of cooking.
5. Once done, serve in a platter drizzled with melted butter, pomegranate seeds and chopped nuts. Taste for seasoning and adjust flavor if needed.

Air-fried Avocado

Preparation Time: **10 minutes**

Cooking Time: **10 minutes**

Yields: 2 servings

Ingredients

- ½ cup all-purpose flour
- 2 avocados
- 2 large eggs
- 2 tbsps. canola mayonnaise
- 1 tbsp. apple cider vinegar
- 1 tbsp. Sriracha chili sauce
- 1½ tsps. black pepper
- ¼ tsp. Kosher salt
- ½ cup Panko bread crumbs
- ¼ cup no-salt-added ketchup
- 1 tbsp. water
- Cooking spray

Directions

1. Cut avocados into 4 wedges each. Prepare 3 shallow dishes.
2. In the first shallow dish, combine avocado wedges with flour and pepper.
3. In another dish, lightly beat eggs.
4. Place bread crumbs in the third dish.

5. First, dredge avocado wedges in the flour mixture, one after the other. After coating with flour, shake lightly to remove excess flour and dip the avocado to the egg mixture, likewise shaking lightly to drip off excess liquid. Finally, dip each wedge to the bread crumbs coating them evenly on all sides and spray with cooking oil.

6. Arrange avocado wedges in the instant pot duo air fryer basket, place inside the pot, and cover with the air fryer lid. Set to air fry at 400 degrees F until wedges turn golden brown, turning them over halfway through cooking. Remove avocado wedges from the fryer and sprinkle them with salt.

7. Meanwhile, while waiting for the avocado wedges to get cooked, mix mayonnaise, ketchup, apple cider vinegar, water and Sriracha sauce in a small bowl.

8. Serve the prepared sauce with the avocado wedges while still warm.

Mediterranean Veggies

Preparation Time: **5 minutes**

Cooking Time: **20 minutes**

Yields: 4 servings

Ingredients

- 1 large courgette
- 2 oz. cherry tomatoes
- 1 green pepper
- 1 medium carrot
- 1 large parsnip
- 1 tsp. mixed herbs
- 2 tbsps. honey
- 3 tbsps. olive oil
- 2 tsps. garlic puree
- 1 tsp. mustard
- Salt and pepper to taste

Directions

1. Slice up the courgette and the green pepper.
2. Peel and dice the carrot and the parsnip.
3. Add them all altogether in the air fryer basket of the instant pot duo along with raw cherry tomatoes, herbs, garlic puree, mustard, salt and pepper. Drizzle with three tablespoons of olive oil.

4. Place the air fryer in the pot and air fry for 15 minutes at 356 degrees F using the instant pot duo crisp air fryer. Sprinkle with more salt if needed and serve.

Rosemary Air-fried Potatoes

Preparation Time: **10 minutes**

Cooking Time: **15 minutes**

Yields: 4 servings

Ingredients

- 3 tbsps. vegetable oil
- 4 yellow baby potatoes, quartered
- 2 tsps. dried rosemary, minced
- 1 tbsp. minced garlic
- 1 tsp. ground black pepper
- ¼ cup chopped parsley
- 1 tbsp. fresh lime or lemon juice
- 1 tsp. salt

Directions

1. Add potatoes, garlic, rosemary, oil, pepper, and salt in a large bowl. Mix thoroughly.
2. Arrange seasoned potatoes in the air fryer basket and place inside the instant pot duo. Cover with the air fryer lid and air-fry at 400 degrees F for about 15 minutes.
3. Check to see if potatoes are cooked through.
4. Once cooked, take it out of the air fryer and place in a platter.
5. Sprinkle with lemon juice and parsley.
6. Serve warm.

Nutritional Information (as per serving): Calories – 201 kcal; Fat – 10.71g; Carbohydrates – 22.71g; Protein –3.34g; sugar –1.32g; Fiber – 3.5g; Sodium – 592.97mg

Air Fried Cauliflower Rice

Preparation Time: **10 minutes**

Cooking Time: **15 minutes**

Yields: 2 servings

Ingredients

- 2 cups cauliflower florets
- 3 cloves of garlic
- ½ tsp. smoked paprika
- 1 tbsp. peanut oil

Directions

1. Smash garlic using the blade of a knife.

2. Place all ingredients in a mixing bowl and mix to coat cauliflower florets with the seasoning.

3. Line the air fryer basket with parchment paper and place coated florets in it.

4. Insert the basket inside the instant pot duo crisp and attach the Air Fryer Lid.

5. Air fry for 15 minutes at 400 degrees F, shaking the air fryer basket every 5 minutes. If you want it crispier, cook for an additional 5 minutes.

6. Serve and enjoy!

Nutritional Information (as per serving): Calories – 129.8 kcal; Carbohydrates – 12.4g; Fat – 7 g; Protein – 4.3 g; Sugar – 5 g; Sodium –642 mg

Chapter 6 :

Fish And Seafood Recipes

Salmon with Capers and Mash

Preparation time: 10 minutes

Cooking time: 20 minutes

Servings: 4

Ingredients:

- 4 salmon fillets, skinless and boneless

- 1 tablespoon capers, drained

- Salt and black pepper to the taste

- Juice from 1 lemon

- 2 teaspoons olive oil

- For the potato mash:

- 2 tablespoons olive oil

- 1 tablespoon dill, dried

- 1 pound potatoes, chopped

- ½ cup milk

Directions:

1. Put potatoes in a pot, add water to cover, add some salt, bring to a boil over medium high heat, cook for 15 minutes, drain, transfer to a bowl, mash with a potato masher, add 2 tablespoons oil, dill, salt, pepper and milk, whisk well and leave aside for now.

2. Season salmon with salt and pepper, drizzle 2 teaspoons oil over them, rub, transfer to your air fryer's basket, add capers on top, cook at 360 degrees F and cook for 8 minutes.

3. Divide salmon and capers on plates, add mashed potatoes on the side, drizzle lemon juice all over and serve.

Enjoy!

Nutrition: calories 300, fat 17, fiber 8, carbs 12, protein 18

Lemony Saba Fish

Preparation time: 10 minutes

Cooking time: 8 minutes

Servings: 1

Ingredients:

- 4 Saba fish fillet, boneless

- Salt and black pepper to the taste

- 3 red chili pepper, chopped

- 2 tablespoons lemon juice

- 2 tablespoon olive oil

- 2 tablespoon garlic, minced

Directions:

1. Season fish fillets with salt and pepper and put in a bowl.

2. Add lemon juice, oil, chili and garlic toss to coat, transfer fish to your air fryer and cook at 360 degrees F for 8 minutes, flipping halfway.

3. Divide among plates and serve with some fries.

Enjoy!

Nutrition: calories 300, fat 4, fiber 8, carbs 15, protein 15

Asian Halibut

Preparation time: 30 minutes

Cooking time: 10 minutes

Servings: 3

Ingredients:

- 1 pound halibut steaks

- 2/3 cup soy sauce

- ¼ cup sugar

- 2 tablespoons lime juice

- ½ cup mirin

- ¼ teaspoon red pepper flakes, crushed

- ¼ cup orange juice

- ¼ teaspoon ginger, grated

- 1 garlic clove, minced

Directions:

1. Put soy sauce in a pan, heat up over medium heat, add mirin, sugar, lime and orange juice, pepper flakes, ginger and garlic, stir well, bring to a boil and take off heat.

2. Transfer half of the marinade to a bowl, add halibut, toss to coat and leave aside in the fridge for 30 minutes.

3. Transfer halibut to your air fryer and cook at 390 degrees F for 10 minutes, flipping once.

4. Divide halibut steaks on plates, drizzle the rest of the marinade all over and serve hot.

Enjoy!

Nutrition: calories 286, fat 5, fiber 12, carbs 14, protein 23

Cod and Vinaigrette

Preparation time: 10 minutes

Cooking time: 15 minutes

Servings: 4

Ingredients:

- 4 cod fillets, skinless and boneless

- 12 cherry tomatoes, halved

- 8 black olives, pitted and roughly chopped

- 2 tablespoons lemon juice

- Salt and black pepper to the taste

- 2 tablespoons olive oil

- Cooking spray

- 1 bunch basil, chopped

Directions:

1. Season cod with salt and pepper to the taste, place in your air fryer's basket and cook at 360 degrees F for 10 minutes, flipping after 5 minutes.

2. Meanwhile, heat up a pan with the oil over medium heat, add tomatoes, olives and lemon juice, stir, bring to a simmer, add basil, salt and pepper, stir well and take off heat.

3. Divide fish on plates and serve with the vinaigrette drizzled on top.

Enjoy!

Nutrition: calories 300, fat 5, fiber 8, carbs 12, protein 8

Shrimp and Crab Mix

Preparation time: 10 minutes

Cooking time: 25 minutes

Servings: 4

Ingredients:

- ½ cup yellow onion, chopped

- 1 cup green bell pepper, chopped

- 1 cup celery, chopped

- 1 pound shrimp, peeled and deveined

- 1 cup crabmeat, flaked

- 1 cup mayonnaise

- 1 teaspoon Worcestershire sauce

- Salt and black pepper to the taste

- 2 tablespoons breadcrumbs

- 1 tablespoon butter, melted

- 1 teaspoon sweet paprika

Directions:

1. In a bowl, mix shrimp with crab meat, bell pepper, onion, mayo, celery, salt, pepper and Worcestershire sauce, toss well.

2. Sprinkle bread crumbs and paprika, add melted butter, place in your air fryer and cook at 320 degrees F for 25 minutes, shaking halfway.

3. Divide among plates and serve right away.

Enjoy!

Nutrition: calories 200, fat 13, fiber 9, carbs 17, protein 19

Seafood Casserole

Preparation time: 10 minutes

Cooking time: 40 minutes

Servings: 6

Ingredients:

- 6 tablespoons butter

- 2 ounces mushrooms, chopped

- 1 small green bell pepper, chopped

- 1 celery stalk, chopped

- 2 garlic cloves, minced

- 1 small yellow onion, chopped

- Salt and black pepper to the taste

- 4 tablespoons flour

- ½ cup white wine

- 1 and ½ cups milk

- ½ cup heavy cream

- 4 sea scallops, sliced

- 4 ounces haddock, skinless, boneless and cut into small pieces 4 ounces lobster meat, already cooked and cut into small pieces ½ teaspoon mustard powder

- 1 tablespoon lemon juice

- 1/3 cup bread crumbs

- Salt and black pepper to the taste

- 3 tablespoons cheddar cheese, grated

- A handful parsley, chopped

- 1 teaspoon sweet paprika

Directions:

1. Heat up a pan with 4 tablespoons butter over medium high heat, add bell pepper, mushrooms, celery, garlic, onion and wine, stir and cook for 10 minutes

2. Add flour, cream and milk, stir well and cook for 6 minutes.

3. Add lemon juice, salt, pepper, mustard powder, scallops, lobster meat and haddock, stir well, take off heat and transfer to a pan that fits your air fryer.

4. In a bowl, mix the rest of the butter with bread crumbs, paprika and cheese and sprinkle over seafood mix.

5. Transfer pan to your air fryer and cook at 360 degrees F for 16 minutes.

6. Divide among plates and serve with parsley sprinkled on top.

Enjoy!

Nutrition: calories 270, fat 32, fiber 14, carbs 15, protein 23

Trout Fillet and Orange Sauce

Preparation time: 10 minutes

Cooking time: 10 minutes

Servings: 4

Ingredients:

- 4 trout fillets, skinless and boneless

- 4 spring onions, chopped

- 1 tablespoon olive oil

- 1 tablespoon ginger, minced

- Salt and black pepper to the taste

- Juice and zest from 1 orange

Directions:

1. Season trout fillets with salt, pepper, rub them with the olive oil, place in a pan add ginger, green onions, orange zest and juice, toss well, place in your air fryer and cook at 360 degrees F for 10 minutes.

2. Divide fish and sauce on plates and serve right away.

Enjoy!

Nutrition: calories 239, fat 10, fiber 7, carbs 18, protein 23

Battered & Crispy Fish Tacos

Preparation: 10minutes

Cooking time: 10 minutes

Servings: 2

Ingredients:

- 11/2 cup Flour Corn tortillas Peach salsa Cilantro

- Fresh halibut, slice into strips

- 1 can of beer

- 2 tablespoons Vegetable Oil

- 1 teaspoon baking powder

- 1 teaspoon Salt Cholula sauce Avocado Cream (recipe below)

Directions:

1. Lay out the corn tortillas topped with peach salsa on a plate and set aside.

2. Combine 1 cup of flour, beer and baking powder until it forms a pancake like consistency.

3. Toss the fish in the remaining flour then dip in the beer batter mixture until well coated.

4. Place on preheated Air Fryer rack and cook 6-8 minutes or until golden at 200°F.

5. Place the fish on top of the salsa mixture topped with avocado cream, cilantro and Cholula sauce.

6. To Make The Avocado Cream:

7. 1 large avocado 3/4 cup buttermilk Juice from 1/2 lime Combine in a blender until smooth.

Steamed Salmon & Dill Dip

Preparation: 15 minutes

Cooking time: 10 minutes

Servings: 2

Ingredients:

- ¾ pound of salmon, cut in half

- 8 tablespoons of sour cream

- 2 teaspoons of olive oil

- 6 teaspoons of finely chopped dill

- 8 tablespoons of Greek Yogurt

- ¼ teaspoons of salt

Directions:

1. Heat your Air Fryer to 285°F. Add a cup of cool water at the base of your Air Fryer.

2. Coat each portion of the salmon with olive oil and season with salt.

3. Place into the fryer basket and cook for about 11 minutes.

4. While cooking the fish, mix the sour cream, salt, yogurt and dill in a bowl.

5. Remove the fish from the Air Fryer and garnish with a pinch of dill and serve with the dill dip.

Salmon And Potato Fishcakes

Preparation: 63 minutes

Cooking time: 7 minutes

Servings: 4

Ingredients:

- 14 ounces of potatoes, cooked and mashed

- 4 tablespoons of chopped parsley

- ½ pound of salmon, cooked and shredded

- ¼ cup of flour

- 1 ounce of capers

- 1 lemon zest Salt and pepper to taste Oil spray

Directions:

1. Mix the mashed potatoes with the salmon, capers, parsley and zest. Add salt and pepper and mix thoroughly.

2. Mold into cakes and coat with flour. Refrigerate for an hour until firm.

3. Preheat the Air Fryer to 356°F.

4. Put the fishcakes into the air fryer basket, spray oil on them and bake for about 7 minutes.

Crab And Vegetable Croquettes

Preparation: 30 minutes

Cooking time: 20 minutes

Servings: 6

Ingredients:

- 4 tablespoons of finely chopped bell pepper

- 4 tablespoons of mayonnaise

- 4 tablespoons of finely chopped onions

- 4 tablespoons of sour cream

- 16 ounces of lump crabmeat

- 1 teaspoon of vegetable oil

- ½ teaspoon of lemon juice

- ½ teaspoon of salt

- ½ teaspoon of finely chopped parsley

- ½ teaspoon of ground pepper

- 2 egg whites

- 6 teaspoons of finely chopped celery

- ¼ teaspoon of finely chopped tarragon

- ¼ teaspoon of finely chopped chives

- 1 cup of breadcrumbs

- 1 cup of flour

Directions:

1. Mix the onions, vegetable oil, celery and peppers in a pot and place over medium heat. Sweat for 5 minutes until translucent. Turn off heat and set aside to cool.

2. Transfer the mixture into a mixing bowl and add the crabmeat, chives, tarragon, mayonnaise, ground pepper, lemon juice, sour cream, and parsley. Mix thoroughly and mold into small balls.

3. Heat your Air Fryer to 390°F.

4. Mix the breadcrumbs and salt together and set aside. Put the egg white and flour into separate bowls.

5. Put the molded balls into the flour, then dip into egg whites and finally roll them in the breadcrumbs to coat evenly.

6. Place half of the balls in the fryer basket and cook for 10 minutes until golden. Do same for the second batch until all the croquettes are cooked.

Coconut Coated Fish Cakes With Mango Sauce

Preparation: 20 minutes

 Cooking time: 14 minutes

Servings: 4

Ingredients:

- 18 ounces of white fish fillet

- 1 green onion, finely chopped

- 1 mango, peeled, cubed

- 4 tablespoons of ground coconut

- 1½ ounces of parsley, finely chopped

- 1½ teaspoons of ground fresh red chili

- 1 lime, juice and zest

- 1 egg

- 1 teaspoon of salt

Directions:

1. Add ½ ounce of parsley, ½ teaspoon of ground chili, half of the lime juice and zest to the mango cubes and mix thoroughly.

2. Using a food processor, puree the fish and add the salt, egg, and the rest of the lime zest, lime juice and chili. Stir in the green onions, 2 tablespoons of coconut and the rest of the parsley.

121

3. Put the rest of the coconut in a shallow dish. Mold the fish mixture into 12 round cakes. Place the cakes in the coconut to coat them.

4. Put half of the cakes into the fryer basket and bake for 7 minutes at 356°F. Remove when cakes are golden and bake the second batch of cakes.

5. Serve the cakes with the mango salsa.

Chapter 7 :

Desserts Recipes

Cream Egg Whites Cake

Preparation Time: 5 minutes

Cooking Time: 30 minutes

Servings: 12

Ingredients:

- ¼ cup butter, melted

- 1 cup powdered erythritol

- One teaspoon strawberry extract

- 12 egg whites

- Two teaspoons cream of tartar

- A pinch of salt

Directions:

1. Place the instant pot air fryer lid on and preheat the instant pot at 3900F for 5 minutes.

2. Mix the egg whites and cream of tartar.

3. Use a hand mixer and whisk until white and fluffy.

4. Put the rest of the ingredients except for the butter and whisk for another minute. Pour into a baking dish and place in the instant pot.

5. The air fryer should close the lid and cook for 30 minutes at 4000F.

6. Drizzle with melted butter once cooled.

Nutrition: Calories per serving: 65; Carbs: 1.8g; Protein: 3.1g; Fat: 5g

Banana-baking Powder Brownies

Preparation Time: 5 minutes

Cooking Time: 30 minutes

Servings: 12

Ingredients:

- 2 cups almond flour

- Two teaspoons baking powder

- ½ teaspoon baking soda

- ½ teaspoon salt

- One over-ripe banana

- Three large eggs

- ½ teaspoon stevia powder

- ¼ cup of coconut oil

- One tablespoon vinegar

- 1/3 cup cocoa powder

Directions:

1. Place the instant pot air fryer lid on and preheat the instant pot at 3500F for 5 minutes.

2. Mixing all ingredients in a food processor and pulse until well combined.

3. Pour into a baking dish that will fit in the instant pot.

4. Place the baking dish in the instant pot and close the air fryer lid.

5. Cook for 30 minutes at 3500F or if a toothpick inserted in the middle comes out clean.

Nutrition: Calories per serving: 75; Carbs: 2.1g; Protein: 1.7g; Fat: 6.6g

Cherries 'n Almond Flour Bars

Preparation Time: 5 minutes

Cooking Time: 30 minutes

Servings: 12

Ingredients:

- ¼ cup of water

- ½ cup butter softened

- ½ teaspoon salt

- ½ teaspoon vanilla

- 1 ½ cups almond flour

- 1 cup erythritol

- 1 cup fresh cherries, pitted

- One tablespoon xanthan gum

- Two eggs

Directions:

1. Shallow bowl, mixing all the first six ingredients until you form a dough.

2. Press the dough in a baking dish that will fit in the instant pot. Place the baking dish in the instant pot.

3. The air fryer should close the lid and cook for 10 minutes at 3750F.

4. Meanwhile, mix the cherries, water, and xanthan gum in a bowl.

5. Take the dough out and pour over the cherry mixture.

6. Return to the instant pot and cook for 25 minutes more at 3750F.

Nutrition: Calories per serving: 99; Carbs: 2.1g; Protein: 1.8g; Fat: 9.3g

Chocolate Chip with Walnut Mug

Preparation Time: 5 minutes

Cooking Time: 20 minutes

Servings: 6

Ingredients:

- ¼ cup walnuts, shelled and chopped

- ½ cup butter, unsalted

- ½ cup dark chocolate chips

- ½ cup erythritol

- ½ teaspoon baking soda

- ½ teaspoon salt

- One tablespoon vanilla extract

- 2 ½ cups almond flour

- Two large eggs, beaten

Directions:

1. Place the instant pot air fryer lid on and preheat the instant pot at 3700F for 5 minutes.

2. Combine all ingredients in a mixing bowl.

3. Place in greased mugs and place the mugs in the instant pot.

4. The air fryer and cook for 20 minutes at 3750F.

Nutrition: Calories per serving: 234; Carbs: 4.9g; Protein: 2.3g; Fat: 22.8g

Choco-peanut Mug Cake

Preparation Time: 5 minutes

Cooking Time: 20 minutes

Servings: 1

Ingredients:

- ¼ teaspoon baking powder

- ½ teaspoon vanilla extract

- One egg

- One tablespoon heavy cream

- One tablespoon peanut butter

- One teaspoon butter softened

- Two tablespoon erythritol

- Two tablespoons cocoa powder, unsweetened

Directions:

1. Place the instant pot air fryer lid on and preheat the instant pot at 3900F for 5 minutes.

2. Combine all ingredients in a mixing bowl.

3. Pour into a greased mug and place in the instant pot.

4. The air fryer lid and cook for 20 minutes at 4000F or if a toothpick inserted in the middle comes out clean.

Nutrition: Calories per serving: 293 Carbs:8.5g Protein: 12.4g Fat: 23.3g

Coconut Flakes Bars

Preparation Time: 10 minutes

Cooking Time: 20 minutes

Servings: 3

Ingredients:

- ¼ cup almond flour

- ¼ cup of coconut oil

- ¼ cup dried coconut flakes

- ¼ teaspoon salt

- ½ cup lime juice

- ¾ cup coconut flour

- One ¼ cup erythritol powder

- One tablespoon lime zest

- Four eggs

Directions:

1. Place the instant pot air fryer lid on and preheat the instant pot at 3750F for 5 minutes.

2. Combine all ingredients in a mixing bowl.

3. Place in a greased mug and place the mug in the instant pot.

4. The air fryer lid and cook for 20 minutes at 3750F.

Nutrition: Calories per serving: 506; Carbs: 21.9g; Protein: 19.3g; Fat: 37.9g

Almond Coconut Vanilla Bombs

Preparation Time: 5 minutes

Cooking Time: 15 minutes

Servings: 12

Ingredients:

- ¼ cup almond flour

- ½ cup shredded coconut

- One tablespoon coconut oil

- One tablespoon vanilla extract

- Two tablespoons liquid stevia

- Three egg whites

Directions:

1. Place the instant pot air fryer lid on and preheat the instant pot at 3900F for 5 minutes.

2. Combine all ingredients in a mixing bowl.

3. Form small balls using your hands.

4. Place in an air fryer basket in the instant pot.

5. The air fryer lid and cook for 15 minutes at 4000F.

Nutrition: Calories per serving: 23; Carbs: 0.7g; Protein: 1.1g; Fat: 1.8g

Coconut Cashew-powder Bars

Preparation Time: 5 minutes

Cooking Time: 25 minutes

Servings: 12

Ingredients:

- ¼ cup cashew

- ¼ cup fresh lemon juice, freshly squeezed

- ¾ cup of coconut milk

- ¾ cup erythritol

- 1 cup desiccated coconut

- 1 teaspoon baking powder

- Two eggs, beaten

- Two tablespoons coconut oil

- A dash of salt

Directions:

1. Place the instant pot air fryer lid on and preheat the instant pot at 3500F for 5 minutes.

2. In a mixing bowl, combine all ingredients.

3. Use a hand mixer to mix everything.

4. Pour into a baking dish that will fit in the instant pot. Place the baking dish in the instant pot.

5. The air fryer lid and cook for 25 minutes at 3500F or until a toothpick inserted in the middle come out clean.

Nutrition: Calories per serving: 118; Carbs: 3.9g; Protein: 2.6g; Fat:10.2g

Egg Cream Cheese Cookie

Preparation Time: 5 minutes

Cooking Time: 20 minutes

Servings: 12

Ingredients:

- ¼ cup butter

- ¼ teaspoon xanthan gum

- ½ teaspoon coffee espresso powder

- ½ teaspoon stevia powder

- ¾ cup almond flour

- One egg

- One teaspoon vanilla

- 1/3 cup sesame seeds

- Two tablespoons cocoa powder

- Two tablespoons cream cheese softened

Directions:

1. Place the instant pot air fryer lid on and preheat the instant pot at 3900F for 5 minutes.

2. Combine all ingredients in a mixing bowl.

139

3. Press into a baking dish that will fit in the instant pot. Place the baking dish in the instant pot.

4. The air fryer lid and cook for 20 minutes at 4000F or if a toothpick inserted in the middle comes out clean.

Nutrition: Calories per serving: 88; Carbs: 1.3g; Protein: 1.9g; Fat: 8.3g

Crispy Buttered Oat Peaches

Preparation Time: 5 minutes

Cooking Time: 30 minutes

Servings: 4

Ingredients:

- 1 teaspoon cinnamon

- 1/3 cup oats, dry rolled

- Two tablespoon flour, white

- Three tablespoon butter, unsalted

- Three tablespoon sugar

- Three tablespoon pecans, chopped

- 4 cup sliced peaches, frozen

Directions:

1. Place the instant pot air fryer lid on and lightly grease baking pan of the instant pot with cooking spray. Mix in a tsp cinnamon, 2 tbsp flour, 3 tbsp sugar, and peaches. Place in the instant pot.

2. The air fryer lid and cook for 20 minutes at 3000F.

3. Mix the rest of the ingredients in a bowl. Pour over peaches.

4. Cook for another 10 minutes at 3000F.

5. Serve and enjoy.

Nutrition: Calories per serving: 435; Carbs: 74.1g; Protein: 4.3g; Fat: 13.4g

Easy Baked Chocolate Mug Cake

Preparation Time: 8 minutes

Cooking Time: 15 minutes

Servings: 3

Ingredients:

- ½ cup of cocoa powder

- ½ cup stevia powder

- 1 cup coconut cream

- One package cream cheese, room temperature

- One tablespoon vanilla extract

- Four tablespoons butter

Directions:

1. Place the instant pot air fryer lid on and preheat the instant pot at 3500F for 5 minutes.

2. In a mixing bowl, combine all ingredients.

3. Using a hand mixer to mix everything until fluffy.

4. Pour into greased mugs.

5. Place the mugs in the instant pot.

6. The air fryer should close the lid and cook for 15 minutes at 3500F.

7. Enjoy and serve it.

Nutrition: Calories per serving: 744; Carbs:15.3 g; Protein: 13.9g; Fat: 69.7g

Egg and Coconut 'n Cocoa Buns

Preparation Time: 5 minutes

Cooking Time: 15 minutes

Servings: 8

Ingredients:

- ¼ cup cacao nibs

- 1 cup of coconut milk

- 1/3 cup coconut flour

- Three tablespoons cacao powder

- Four eggs, beaten

Directions:

1. Place the instant pot air fryer lid on and preheat the instant pot at 3750F for 5 minutes.

2. Combine all ingredients in a mixing bowl.

3. Form buns using your hands and place in a baking dish that will fit in the instant pot.

4. The air fryer lid and cook for 15 minutes for 3750F.

Nutrition: Calories per serving: 161; Carbs: 4g; Protein: 5.7g; Fat: 13.6g

Cocoa-egg Doughnut Recipe

Preparation Time: 5 minutes

Cooking Time: 20 minutes

Servings: 4

Ingredients:

- ¼ cup of coconut milk

- ¼ cup erythritol

- ¼ cup flaxseed meal

- ¾ cup almond flour

- One tablespoon cocoa powder

- One teaspoon vanilla extract

- Two large eggs, beaten

- Three tablespoons coconut oil

Directions:

1. Place all ingredients in a mixing bowl.

2. Mix until well combined.

3. Scoop the dough into individual doughnut moulds.

4. Place the instant pot air fryer lid on and preheat the instant pot at 3500F for 5 minutes.

5. Place moulds in an air fryer basket in the instant pot.

6. The air fryer lid and cook for 20 minutes at 3500F, cook in batches if possible.

Nutrition: Calories per serving: 222; Carbs: 5.1g; Protein: 3.9g; Fat: 20.7g

Chocolate-almond Flour Cake with Egg

Preparation Time: 5 minutes

Cooking Time: 15 minutes

Servings: 4

Ingredients:

- ¼ cup coconut oil, melted
- ¼ teaspoon vanilla powder
- 1 cup dark chocolate powder
- One tablespoon almond flour
- Two tablespoons stevia powder
- Three large eggs, beaten

Directions:

1. Place the instant pot air fryer lid on and preheat the instant pot at 3750F for 5 minutes.
2. Combine all ingredients in a mixing bowl.
3. The ramekins grease with coconut oil and dust with chocolate powder.
4. Pour the batter into the ramekins and place in the instant pot.
5. Close the air fryer lid and cook at 3750F for 15 minutes.

Nutrition: Calories per serving: 251; Carbs: 14.5g; Protein: 4.1g; Fat: 19.6g

Oriental Coconut Cake

Preparation Time: 10 minutes

Cooking Time: 40 minutes

Servings: 8

Ingredients:

- 1 cup gluten-free flour

- Two eggs

- 1/2 cup flaked coconut

- 1 1/2 teaspoons baking powder

- 1/2 teaspoon baking soda

- 1/2 teaspoon xanthan gum

- 1/2 teaspoon salt

- 1/2 cup coconut milk

- 1/2 cup vegetable oil

- 1/2 teaspoon vanilla extract

- 1/4 cup chopped walnuts

- 3/4 cup white sugar

Directions:

1. In a blender, blend all wet ingredients. Add dry ingredients and blend thoroughly.

2. Place the instant pot air fryer lid on and lightly grease baking pan of the instant pot with cooking spray. Pour in batter.

3. Cover the pan with foil and place the baking pan in the instant pot.

4. The air fryer lid and cook for 30 minutes at 3300F.

5. Let it rest for 10 minutes

6. Serve and enjoy.

Nutrition:Calories per serving: 359; Carbs: 35.2g; Protein: 4.3g; Fat: 22.3g

Pound Cake with Fresh Apples

Preparation Time: 15 minutes

Cooking Time: 60 minutes

Servings: 6

Ingredients:

- 1 cup white sugar

- One teaspoon vanilla extract

- One medium Granny Smith apples - peeled, cored and chopped

- One egg

- 1/2 cup all-purpose flour

- 1/2 teaspoon baking soda

- 1/2 teaspoon salt

- 1/4 teaspoon ground cinnamon

- 2/3 cup and one tablespoon chopped walnuts

- 3/4 cup vegetable oil

Directions:

1. In a blender, blend all ingredients except for apples and walnuts. Blend thoroughly. Fold in apples and walnuts.

2. Place the instant pot air fryer lid on, lightly grease baking pan of the instant pot with cooking spray. Pour batter.

151

3. Cover the pan with foil and place the baking pan int the instant pot.

4. The air fryer lid and cook for 30 minutes at 3300F.

5. The foil should remove and cook for another 20 minutes.

6. Let it stand for 10 minutes.

7. Serve and enjoy.

Nutrition:Calories per Serving: 696; Carbs: 71.1g; Protein: 6.5g; Fat: 42.8g

Coconut-raspberry Cake

Preparation Time: 5 minutes

Cooking Time: 20 minutes

Servings: 12

Ingredients:

- ¼ cup of coconut oil

- 1 cup of coconut milk

- 1 cup raspberries, pulsed

- One teaspoon vanilla bean

- 1/3 cup erythritol powder

- 3 cups desiccated coconut

Directions:

1. Place the instant pot air fryer lid on and preheat the instant pot at 3750F for 5 minutes.

2. Combine all ingredients in a mixing bowl.

3. Pour into a greased baking dish. Place the baking dish in the instant pot.

4. Close the air fryer lid and cook for 20 minutes at 3750F.

Nutrition: Calories per serving: 132; Carbohydrates: 9.7g; Protein: 1.5g; Fat: 9.7g

Egg-vanilla Bean Cake

Preparation Time: 15 minutes

Cooking Time: 30 minutes

Servings: 12

Ingredients:

- ¼ teaspoon salt

- ½ cup erythritol powder

- One vanilla bean scraped

- 1/3 cup water

- 2/3 cup butter, melted

- Four large eggs

Directions:

1. Place the instant pot air fryer lid on and preheat the instant pot at 3750F for 5 minutes.

2. Combine all ingredients in a mixing bowl.

3. Pour into a greased baking dish. Place the baking dish in the instant pot.

4. Close the air fryer lid and cook for 30 minutes at 3750F.

Nutrition: Calories per serving: 126; Carbohydrates: 2.3g; Protein: 1.6g; Fat: 12.3g

Yummy Banana Cookies

Preparation Time: 5 minutes

Cooking Time: 10 minutes

Servings: 6

Ingredients:

- 1 cup dates, pitted and chopped

- One teaspoon vanilla

- 1/3 cup vegetable oil

- 2 cups rolled oats

- Three ripe bananas

Directions:

1. Place the instant pot air fryer lid on and preheat the instant pot at 3500F.

2. In a shallow bowl, mash the bananas and add in the rest of the ingredients.

3. Let it rest inside the fridge for 10 minutes.

4. Drop a teaspoonful on cut parchment paper.

5. Place the cookies on the baking dish with parchment paper inside the instant pot. Make sure that the cookies do not overlap.

6. The air fryer lid and cook for 20 minutes or until the edges are crispy.

7. Serve with almond milk.

Nutrition: Calories per serving: 382; Carbohydrates: 50.14g; Protein: 6.54g; Fat: 17.2g

Almond Butter Brownies

Preparation Time: 5 minutes

Cooking Time: 15 minutes

Servings: 4

Ingredients:

- Almond butter – 1/2 cup

- Vanilla – 1/2 tsp.

- Almond milk – 1 tbsp.

- Coconut sugar – 2 tbsps.

- Applesauce – 2 tbsps.

- Honey – 2 tbsps.

- Baking powder – 1/4 tsp.

- Baking soda – 1/2 tsp.

- Cocoa powder – 2 tbsps.

- Almond flour – 3 tbsps.

- Coconut oil – 1 tbsp.

- Sea salt – 1/4 tsp.

Directions:

1. Spray baking pan with cooking spray and set aside. Add coconut oil and almond butter into the microwave-safe bowl and microwave until melted. Stir. Add honey, milk, coconut sugar, vanilla, and applesauce into the melted coconut oil mixture and stir well. Add flour mixture and stir to combine. Pour batter into the baking pan. Place steam rack into the instant pot. Place a baking pan on top of the steam rack. Seal pot with the air fryer lid. Select bake mode and cook at 350 F for 15 minutes. Serve.

Nutrition:Per Serving: Calories 170, Carbs 22g, Fat 8g, Protein 2g

Brownie Muffins

Preparation Time: 5 minutes

Cooking Time: 15 minutes

Servings: 6

Ingredients:

- Cocoa powder – 1/4 cup

- Almond butter – 1/2 cup

- Pumpkin puree – 1 cup

- Liquid stevia – 8 drops

- Protein powder – 2 scoops

Directions:

Add all ingredients into the mixing bowl and beat until smooth. Pour batter into the six silicone muffin moulds. Place the dehydrating tray into the multi-level air fryer basket and place the basket into the instant pot. Place muffin moulds on a dehydrating plate. Seal pot with the air fryer lid. Select bake mode and cook at 350 F for 15 minutes. Serve.

Nutrition: Per Serving: Calories 70, Carbs 6g, Fat 2g, Protein 8g

Oatmeal-Carrot Cookie Cups

PREP 10 minutes / **COOK** 8 to 10 minutes / **MAKES** 16 cups

350°F

PER SERVING (1 cookie cup) Calories: 127; Fat: 5g (35% calories from fat); Saturated Fat: 3g; Protein: 2g; Carbohydrates: 20g; Sodium: 88mg; Fiber: 1g; Sugar: 12g; 7% DV vitamin A

Ingredients

3 tablespoons unsalted butter, at room temperature

½ cup quick-cooking oatmeal

⅓ cup whole-wheat pastry flour

½ teaspoon baking soda

¼ cup dried cherries

¼ cup packed brown sugar

1 tablespoon honey

1 egg white

½ teaspoon vanilla extract

⅓ cup finely grated carrot

Directions

1. In a medium bowl, beat the butter, brown sugar, and honey until well combined.

2. Add the egg white, vanilla, and carrot. Beat to combine.

3. Stir in the oatmeal, pastry flour, and baking soda.

4. Stir in the dried cherries.

5. Double up 32 mini muffin foil cups to make 16 cups. Fill each with about 4 teaspoons of dough. Bake the cookie cups, 8 at a time, for 8 to 10 minutes, or until light golden brown and just set. Serve warm.

Delicious Lemon Muffins

Preparation Time: 5 minutes

Cooking Time: 15 minutes

Servings: 6

Ingredients:

- Egg – 1

- Baking powder – 3/4 tsp.

- Lemon zest – 1 tsp., grated

- Sugar – 1/2 cup

- Vanilla – 1/2 tsp.

- Milk – 1/2 cup

- Canola oil – 2 tbsps.

- Baking soda – 1/4 tsp.

- Flour – 1 cup

- Salt – 1/2 tsp.

Directions:

1. In a mixing bowl, beat egg, vanilla, milk, oil, and sugar until creamy. Add remaining ingredients and stir to combine. Pour batter into the six silicone muffin moulds. Place the dehydrating tray into the multi-level air fryer basket and place the basket into the instant pot.

Place muffin moulds on a dehydrating plate. Seal pot with the air fryer lid. Select bake mode and cook at 350 F for 15 minutes. Serve.

Nutrition: Per Serving: Calories 202, Carbs 34g, Fat 6g, Protein 4g

Vanilla Strawberry Soufflé

Preparation Time: 5 minutes

Cooking Time: 15 minutes

Servings: 4

Ingredients:

- Egg whites – 3

- Strawberries – 1 1/2 cups.

- Vanilla – 1/2 tsp.

- Sugar – 1 tbsp.

Directions:

1. Add strawberries, sugar, and vanilla into the blender and blend until smooth. Add egg whites into the bowl and beat until medium peaks form. Add strawberry mixture and fold well. Pour egg mixture into the ramekins. Place the dehydrating tray into the multi-level air fryer basket and place the basket into the instant pot. Place ramekins on the dehydrating plate. Seal pot with the air fryer lid. Select bake mode and cook at 350 F for 15 minutes. Serve.

Nutrition: Per Serving: Calories 50, Carbs 8g, Fat 0.5g, Protein 3g

Healthy Carrot Muffins

Preparation Time: 5 minutes

Cooking Time: 20 minutes

Servings: 4

Ingredients:

- Egg – 1

- Vanilla – 1 tsp.

- Brown sugar – 1/4 cup

- Granulated sugar – 1/4 cup

- Canola oil – 1/2 tbsp.

- Applesauce – 1/4 cup

- All-purpose flour – 1 cup

- Baking powder – 1 1/2 tsp.

- Nutmeg – 1/4 tsp.

- Cinnamon – 1 tsp.

- Grated carrots – 3/4 cup

- Salt – 1/4 tsp.

Directions:

1. Combine all ingredients into a huge bowl and mix until thoroughly combined. Pour batter into six silicone muffin moulds. Place the dehydrating tray into the multi-level air fryer basket and place the basket into the instant pot. Place muffin moulds on the dehydrating plate. Seal pot with the air fryer lid. Select bake mode and cook at 350 F for 20 minutes. Serve.

Nutrition: Per Serving: Calories 165, Carbs 33g, Fat 2g, Protein 3g

Pumpkin Pie Pudding

PREP 10 minutes / **COOK** 12 to 17 minutes / **SERVES** 4

350°F

PER SERVING Calories: 154; Fat: 5g (29% calories from fat); Saturated Fat: 3g; Protein: 3g; Carbohydrates: 26g; Sodium: 39mg; Fiber: 2g; Sugar: 16g; 194% DV vitamin A; 4% DV vitamin C

Ingredients

¼ cup packed brown sugar

3 tablespoons all-purpose flour

1 tablespoon unsalted butter, melted

1 egg

1 cup canned no-salt-added pumpkin purée (not pumpkin pie filling)

2 tablespoons 1 percent milk

1 teaspoon pure vanilla extract

4 low-fat vanilla wafers, crumbled

Directions

1. Spray a 6-by-2-inch pan with nonstick cooking spray and set aside.

2. In a medium bowl, whisk the pumpkin, brown sugar, flour, butter, egg, milk, and vanilla until combined. Pour the pumpkin mixture into the prepared pan.

3. Bake for 12 to 17 minutes, or until the pudding is set and registers 165°F on a thermometer.

4. Remove the pudding from the air fryer and cool on a wire rack.

167

5. To serve, scoop the pudding into bowls and top with vanilla wafer crumbs.

Purple Potato Chips with Chipotle Sauce and Rosemary

PREP 20 minutes / **COOK** 9 to 14 minutes / **SERVES** 6

400°F

PER SERVING Calories: 68; Fat: 1g (13% calories from fat); Saturated Fat: 0g; Protein 4g; Carbohydrates 11g; Sodium 112mg; Fiber 1g; Sugar 2g; 0% DV vitamin A; 17% DV vitamin C

Ingredients

1 cup Greek yogurt

2 chipotle chiles, minced

2 tablespoons adobo sauce

1 teaspoon paprika

1 tablespoon lemon juice

10 purple fingerling potatoes

1 teaspoon olive oil

2 teaspoons minced fresh rosemary leaves

⅛ teaspoon cayenne pepper

¼ teaspoon coarse sea salt

Directions

1. In a medium bowl, combine the yogurt, minced chiles, adobo sauce, paprika, and lemon juice. Mix well and refrigerate.

2. Wash the potatoes and dry them with paper towels. Slice the potatoes lengthwise, as thinly as possible. You can use a mandoline, a vegetable peeler, or a very sharp knife.

3. Combine the potato slices in a medium bowl and drizzle with the olive oil; toss to coat.

4. Cook the chips, in batches, in the air fryer basket, for 9 to 14 minutes. Use tongs to gently rearrange the chips halfway during cooking time.

5. Sprinkle the chips with the rosemary, cayenne pepper, and sea salt. Serve with the chipotle sauce for dipping.

Deep-fried potato chips contain at least 40% calories from fat.

Cinnamon Carrot Cake

Preparation Time: 5 minutes

Cooking Time: 25 minutes

Servings: 4

Ingredients:

- Egg – 1

- Vanilla – 1/2 tsp.

- Cinnamon – 1/2 tsp.

- Sugar – 1/2 cup

- Canola oil – 1/4 cup

- Walnuts – 1/4, chopped

- Baking powder – 1/2 tsp.

- Flour – 1/2 cup

- Grated carrot – 1/4 cup

Directions:

1. In a considerable bowl, beat sugar and oil for 1-2 minutes. Add vanilla, cinnamon, and egg and beat for 30 seconds. Add remaining ingredients and stir to combine. Pour batter into the prepared baking dish. Place steam rack into the instant pot. Place baking dish on top of the steam rack. Seal pot with the air fryer lid. Select bake mode and cook at 350 F for 25 minutes. Serve.

171

Nutrition: Per Serving: Calories 340, Carbs 39g, Fat 19g, Protein 5g

Blueberry Muffins

Preparation Time: 5 minutes

Cooking Time: 20 minutes

Servings: 9

Ingredients:

- Eggs – 2

- Blueberries – 1 1/2 cups

- Yoghurt – 1 cup

- Sugar – 1 cup

- Baking powder – 1 tbsp.

- Flour – 2 cups

- Fresh lemon juice – 2 tsp.

- Lemon zest – 2 tbsps., grated

- Vanilla – 1 tsp.

- Oil – 1/2 cup

- Salt – 1/2 tsp.

Directions:

1. In a shallow container, combine flour, salt, and baking powder. Set aside. In an enormous box, whisk together eggs, lemon juice, lemon zest, vanilla, oil, yoghurt, and sugar. Add flour mixture and blueberries into the egg mixture and fold well. Pour batter into nine silicone

muffin moulds. Place the dehydrating tray into the multi-level air fryer basket and place the basket into the instant pot. Place six muffin moulds on the dehydrating plate. Seal pot with the air fryer lid. Select bake mode and cook at 375 F for 20 minutes. Cook remaining muffins. Serve.

Nutrition:Per Serving: Calories 343, Carbs 50g, Fat 13g, Protein 5.9g

Almond Raspberry Muffins

Preparation Time: 10 minutes

Cooking Time: 35 minutes

Servings: 6

Ingredients:

- Eggs – 2

- Baking powder – 1 tsp.

- Almond meal – 5 oz

- Coconut oil – 2 tbsps.

- Honey – 2 tbsps.

- Raspberries – 3 oz

Directions:

1. In a bowl, mix the almond meal and baking powder. Add honey, eggs, and oil and stir until thoroughly combined. Add raspberries and fold well. Pour batter into the 6-silicone muffin moulds. Place the dehydrating tray into the multi-level air fryer basket and place the basket into the instant pot. Place six muffin moulds on the dehydrating plate. Seal pot with the air fryer lid. Select bake mode and cook at 350 F for 35 minutes. Serve.

Nutrition: Per Serving: Calories 227, Carbs 13g, Fat 17g, Protein 7g

Vegetable Pot Sticker

PREP 12 minutes / **COOK** 11 to 18 minutes / **MAKES** 12 pot stickers

370°F

PER SERVING (3 pot stickers) Calories: 87; Fat: 3g (31% of calories from fat); Saturated Fat: 0g; Protein: 2g; Carbohydrates: 14g; Sodium: 58mg; Fiber: 1g; Sugar: 1g; 5% DV vitamin A; 22% DV vitamin C

Ingredients

2 garlic cloves, minced

2 teaspoons grated fresh ginger

12 gyoza/pot sticker wrappers

2½ teaspoons olive oil, divided

1 cup shredded red cabbage

¼ cup chopped button mushrooms

¼ cup grated carrot

2 tablespoons minced onion

Directions

1. In a 6-by-2-inch pan, combine the red cabbage, mushrooms, carrot, onion, garlic, and ginger. Add 1 tablespoon of water. Place in the air fryer and cook for 3 to 6 minutes, until the vegetables are crisp-tender. Drain and set aside.

2. Working one at a time, place the pot sticker wrappers on a work surface. Top each wrapper with a scant 1 tablespoon of the filling. Fold half of the wrapper over the other half to form a half circle. Dab one edge with water and press both edges together.

3. To another 6-by-2-inch pan, add 1¼ teaspoons of olive oil. Put half of the pot stickers, seam-side up, in the pan. Air-fry for 5 minutes, or until the bottoms are light golden brown. Add 1 tablespoon of water and return the pan to the air fryer.

4. Air-fry for 4 to 6 minutes more, or until hot. Repeat with the remaining pot stickers, remaining 1¼ teaspoons of oil, and another tablespoon of water. Serve immediately.

Honey-Roasted Pears with Ricotta

PREP 7 minutes / **COOK** 18 to 23 minutes / **SERVES** 4

350°F

PER SERVING Calories: 138; Fat: 4g (26% of calories from fat); Saturated Fat: 3g; Protein: 2g; Carbohydrates: 25g; Sodium: 17mg; Fiber: 3g; Sugar: 21g; 3% DV vitamin A; 5% DV vitamin C

Ingredients

2 large Bosc pears, halved and seeded

3 tablespoons honey

1 tablespoon unsalted butter

½ teaspoon ground cinnamon

¼ cup walnuts, chopped

¼ cup part skim low-fat ricotta cheese, divided

Directions

1. In a 6-by-2-inch pan, place the pears cut-side up.

2. In a small microwave-safe bowl, melt the honey, butter, and cinnamon. Brush this mixture over the cut sides of the pears.

3. Pour 3 tablespoons of water around the pears in the pan. Roast the pears for 18 to 23 minutes, or until tender when pierced with a fork and slightly crisp on the edges, basting once with the liquid in the pan.

4. Carefully remove the pears from the pan and place on a serving plate. Drizzle each with some liquid from the pan, sprinkle the walnuts on top, and serve with a spoonful of ricotta cheese.

Caramel Apple Cake

Preparation Time: 25 minutes

Cooking Time: 45 minutes

Servings: 6

Ingredients

Cake:

- 1 cup all-purpose flour

- 1/4 cup almond flour

- 1/4 cup fine cornmeal

- 1 tsp baking powder

- 1/2 tsp baking soda

- 1/4 tsp salt

- 3/4 cup granulated sugar

- 2 eggs

- 2 tbsp honey

- 3/4 cup plain 2% yogurt

- 1/2 cup olive oil

- 2 tsp lemon zest

- 1 tsp vanilla extract

Caramelized Apples:

- 2 tbsp butter

- 1/2 cup granulated sugar

- 2 tbsp Corn syrup

- 1/4 tsp ground cinnamon

- 4 slices apples peeled, cored and cut into 2-inch

- 1/2 cup granulated sugar

- 2 tbsp Corn syrup

- 1/4 tsp ground cinnamon

Directions

1. Cake: Whisk together flour, almond flour, cornmeal, baking powder, baking soda and salt; set aside.

2. In separate bowl, beat together sugar, eggs and honey until light and fluffy. Beat in yogurt, olive oil, lemon zest and vanilla for about 1 minute or until combined. Stir in flour mixture just until combined. Pour batter into parchment paper-lined 8-inch (20 cm) springform pan.

3. Place trivet in Instant Pot Duo Crisp + Air Fryer; place springform pan on top.

4. With the Air Fryer lid on, select Bake at 350°F. Cook for 25 to 30 minutes or until toothpick inserted in center of cake comes out clean. Let stand for 10 minutes.

5. Caramelized Apples: With the Instant Pot Duo Crisp + Air Fryer lid off, select Saute setting and set to Medium Temperature. Melt butter in inner pot; stir in apples, sugar, corn syrup and cinnamon. Cook for 8 to 10 minutes or until apples are tender, saucy and caramelized.

180

6. Cut cake into 6 slices. Serve warm or cold with apple mixture.

Veggie Frittata

PREP 10 minutes / **COOK** 8 to 12 minutes / **SERVES** 4

350°F

PER SERVING Calories: 77; Fat: 3g (35% calories from fat); Saturated Fat: 1g; Protein: 8g; Carbohydrates: 5g; Sodium: 116mg; Fiber: 1g; Sugar: 3g; 14% DV vitamin A; 62% DV vitamin C

Ingredients

½ cup chopped red bell pepper

⅓ cup minced onion

⅓ cup grated carrot

1 teaspoon olive oil

6 egg whites

1 egg

⅓ cup 2 percent milk

1 tablespoon grated Parmesan cheese

Directions

1. In a 6-by-2-inch pan, stir together the red bell pepper, onion, carrot, and olive oil. Put the pan into the air fryer. Cook for 4 to 6 minutes, shaking the basket once, until the vegetables are tender.

2. Meanwhile, in a medium bowl, beat the egg whites, egg, and milk until combined.

3. Pour the egg mixture over the vegetables in the pan. Sprinkle with the Parmesan cheese. Return the pan to the air fryer.

4. Bake for 4 to 6 minutes more, or until the frittata is puffy and set.

5. Cut into 4 wedges and serve.

Chicken Sausages

PREP 15 minutes / **COOK** 8 to 12 minutes / **MAKES** 8 sausage patties

330°F

PER SERVING (1 patty) Calories: 87; Fat: 2g (21% calories from fat); Saturated Fat: 0g; Protein: 14g; Carbohydrates: 5g; Sodium: 27mg; Fiber: 1g; Sugar 4g; 6% DV vitamin C

Ingredients

1 egg white

2 tablespoons apple juice

⅛ teaspoon freshly ground black pepper

1 Granny Smith apple, peeled and finely chopped

⅓ cup minced onion

3 tablespoons ground almonds

2 garlic cloves, minced

1 pound ground chicken breast

Directions

1. In a medium bowl, thoroughly mix the apple, onion, almonds, garlic, egg white, apple juice, and pepper.

2. With your hands, gently work the chicken breast into the apple mixture until combined.

3. Form the mixture into 8 patties. Put the patties into the air fryer basket. You may need to cook them in batches. Air-fry for 8 to 12 minutes, or until the patties reach an internal temperature of 165°F on a meat thermometer. Serve.

The percentage of calories from fat drops from 78 to 21 percent. That's impressive.

Carrot and Cinnamon Muffins

PREP 15 minutes / **COOK** 12 to 17 minutes / **MAKES** 8 muffins

320°F

PER SERVING (1 muffin) Calories: 201; Fat: 7g (31% calories from fat); Saturated Fat: 1g; Protein: 4g; Carbohydrates: 32g; Sodium: 74mg; Fiber: 4g; Sugar: 14g; 32% DV vitamin A; 1% DV vitamin C

Ingredients

1½ cups whole-wheat pastry flour

2 egg whites

⅔ cup almond milk

3 tablespoons safflower oil

1 teaspoon low-sodium baking powder

⅓ cup brown sugar

½ teaspoon ground cinnamon

1 egg

½ cup finely shredded carrots

⅓ cup golden raisins, chopped

Directions

1. In a medium bowl, combine the flour, baking powder, brown sugar, and cinnamon, and mix well.

2. In a small bowl, combine the egg, egg whites, almond milk, and oil and beat until combined. Stir the egg mixture into the dry ingredients just until combined. Don't overbeat; some lumps should be in the batter—that's just fine.

3. Stir the shredded carrot and chopped raisins gently into the batter.

4. Double up 16 foil muffin cups to make 8 cups. Put 4 of the cups into the air fryer and fill ¾ full with the batter.

5. Bake for 12 to 17 minutes or until the tops of the muffins spring back when lightly touched with your finger.

6. Repeat with remaining muffin cups and the remaining batter. Cool the muffins on a wire rack for 10 minutes before serving.

Asparagus and Bell Pepper Strata

PREP 10 minutes / **COOK** 14 to 20 minutes / **SERVES** 4

330°F

PER SERVING Calories: 100; Fat: 2g (18% of calories from fat); Saturated Fat: 0g; Protein: 9g; Carbohydrates: 14g; Sodium: 129mg; Fiber: 3g; Sugar: 5g; 50% DV vitamin A; 65% DV vitamin C

Ingredients

8 large asparagus spears, trimmed and cut into 2-inch pieces

⅓ cup shredded carrot

½ cup chopped red bell pepper

2 slices low-sodium whole-wheat bread, cut into ½-inch cubes

3 egg whites

1 egg

3 tablespoons 1 percent milk

½ teaspoon dried thyme

Directions

1. In a 6-by-2-inch pan, combine the asparagus, carrot, red bell pepper, and 1 tablespoon of water. Bake in the air fryer for 3 to 5 minutes, or until crisp-tender. Drain well.

2. Add the bread cubes to the vegetables and gently toss.

3. In a medium bowl, whisk the egg whites, egg, milk, and thyme until frothy.

4. Pour the egg mixture into the pan. Bake for 11 to 15 minutes, or until the strata is slightly puffy and set and the top starts to brown. Serve.

Pumpkin Donut Holes

PREP 15 minutes / **COOK** 14 minutes / **MAKES** 12 donut holes

360°F

PER SERVING (2 donut holes) Calories: 142; Fat: 4g (25% calories from fat); Saturated Fat: 3g; Protein: 3g; Carbohydrates: 23g; Sodium: 24mg; Fiber: 3g; Sugar: 7g; 45% DV vitamin A

Ingredients

1 cup whole-wheat pastry flour, plus more as needed

3 tablespoons packed brown sugar

½ teaspoon ground cinnamon

1 teaspoon low-sodium baking powder

⅓ cup canned no-salt-added pumpkin purée

3 tablespoons 2 percent milk, plus more as needed

2 tablespoons unsalted butter, melted

1 egg white

Powdered sugar (optional)

Directions

1. In a medium bowl, mix the pastry flour, brown sugar, cinnamon, and baking powder.

2. In a small bowl, beat the pumpkin, milk, butter, and egg white until combined. Add the pumpkin mixture to the dry ingredients and mix until combined. You may need to add more flour or milk to form a soft dough.

3. Divide the dough into 12 pieces. With floured hands, form each piece into a ball.

4. Cut a piece of parchment paper or aluminum foil to fit inside the air fryer basket but about 1 inch smaller in diameter. Poke holes in the paper or foil and place it in the basket.

5. Put 6 donut holes into the basket, leaving some space around each. Air-fry for 5 to 7 minutes, or until the donut holes reach an internal temperature of 200°F and are firm and light golden brown.

6. Let cool for 5 minutes. Remove from the basket and roll in powdered sugar, if desired. Repeat with the remaining donut holes and serve.

Stuffed Apples

PREP 13 minutes / **COOK** 12 to 17 minutes / **SERVES** 4

350°F

PER SERVING Calories: 122; Fat: 4g (29.5% of calories from fat); Saturated Fat: 0g; Protein: 1g; Carbohydrates: 22g; Sodium: 8mg; Fiber: 1g; Sugar: 20g; 5% DV vitamin C

Ingredients

4 medium apples, rinsed and patted dry (see Tip)

2 tablespoons freshly squeezed lemon juice

¼ cup golden raisins

3 tablespoons chopped walnuts

3 tablespoons dried cranberries

2 tablespoons packed brown sugar

⅓ cup apple cider

Directions

1. Cut a strip of peel from the top of each apple and remove the core, being careful not to cut through the bottom of the apple. Sprinkle the cut parts of the apples with lemon juice and place in a 6-by-2-inch pan.

2. In a small bowl, stir together the raisins, walnuts, cranberries, and brown sugar. Stuff one-fourth of this mixture into each apple.

3. Pour the apple cider around the apples in the pan.

Bake in the air fryer for 12 to 17 minutes, or until the apples are tender when pierced with a fork. Serve immediately

Grilled Spiced Fruit

PREP 10 minutes / **COOK** 3 to 5 minutes / **SERVES** 4

400°F

PER SERVING Calories: 121; Fat: 1g (7% calories from fat); Saturated Fat: 0g; Protein: 3g; Carbohydrates: 30g; Sodium: 0mg; Fiber: 4g; Sugar: 25g; 16% DV vitamin A; 27% DV vitamin C

Ingredients

2 peaches, peeled, pitted, and thickly sliced

3 plums, halved and pitted

3 nectarines, halved and pitted

1 tablespoon honey

½ teaspoon ground cinnamon

¼ teaspoon ground allspice

Pinch cayenne pepper

Directions

1. Thread the fruit, alternating the types, onto 8 bamboo or metal skewers that fit into the air fryer.

2. In a small bowl, stir together the honey, cinnamon, allspice, and cayenne. Brush the glaze onto the fruit.

3. Grill the skewers for 3 to 5 minutes, or until lightly browned and caramelized. Cool for 5 minutes and serve.

Conclusion

ou may be no stranger to the Instant Pot. You are probably familiar with the speed with which it cooks. If you knew it quite well, you will realize that it has some other benefits. In case you did not know, the Instant γPot has the following benefits.

1. It Saves Time and Energy

The instant pot has energy efficiency due to the following two major factors, namely:

Its cooking chamber, that is the inner pot, is fully insulated. That is why the cooker does not have to consume much energy before heating up. The second is that you do not have to add much liquid before your meal in the Instant Pot is cooked, it actually boils faster.

Also, when compared to other cooking methods like baking, boiling, roasting, steaming and stovetop, the Instant Pot cooking requires less cook time. So it saves time by up to 70 percent and reduces the energy usage by the same margin. It reaches temperatures above boiling translating to fast cooking.

2. It Requires Less Water

When steaming in an Instant Pot, up to 75% less water is needed compared to other cooking methods. Again, it is also great for energy efficiency because it will require less energy as you will need to heat or boil less water.

3. It Has Intelligent Programming

It has one-touch programs that have been carefully tested and refined based on a series of experiments. Each of the presets has been designed for consistency in cooking results. It is this intelligent programming that ensures cooking is consistent irrespective of the volume and quantities. For instance, it takes the same amount of time to cook one egg and one dozen eggs. You can still have more fine-tuning for most programs. And the Instant Pot can save and remember your setting such as your preference for a shorter or longer.

196

4. It Is Fully Insulated

The Instant Pot cooker base is completely insulated. It has two layers of air pockets situated between the stainless steel exterior and the inner pot. Thus, while the internal temperature exceeds boiling points, the base of the cooker is safe to touch even when the cooking process is long.

This again saves energy as it only heats the inner pot to keep the pressure level. The intelligent programming prevents it from constantly exerting energy in maintaining heat. It engages the element in just 60% of the time during a cook cycle. Thus, it won't heat your home during summertime when you're already struggling with the ferocious heat outside. That means that you will consume less energy on air conditioning.

5. It Retains Vitamins and Nutrients

When you boil or even steam your food in the normal fashion, the water-soluble vitamins will leach out of it. This process reduces the nutritional value of your food. But an instant pot cooks deeply, evenly, and quickly thus allowing your food to retain as much as 90 percent of the water-soluble vitamin contents. This preservation of nutrition may also be due to the limit of its temperatures which maxes somewhere around 250°F (121°C). So it makes your meals healthier. Due to the advanced tech of its embedded microprocessor, you have the total control of your cooking cycles to prepare delicious meals.

6. It Preserves Food's Appearance and Taste

You notice that when you cook in a container that exposes its content, even the one with a lid, your food is exposed to oxygen and heat. This alters the color of the food and reduces its flavor. But the airtight Instant Pot environment saturates your foods with steam which allows the retention and preservation of colors, phytochemicals, and flavors as all are trapped inside their respective ingredients.

7. It Eliminates Harmful Microorganisms

The Instant Pot allows your water to boil beyond 212°F (100°C), thereby guaranteeing the destruction of harmful bacteria in your food. Thus, it is good water treatment. That is why it is advisable to use it as a sort of sterilization tool for baby bottles or jars.

8. It Is Convenient

Thanks to Instant Pot's preset Smart Programs features, it is convenient for the following:

§ Beans and chili

§ Congee/Porridge

§ Keep warm

§ Meat and stew

§ Multigrain

§ Rice

§ Sauté/Browning

§ Slow Cook

§ Soup

§ Steaming

§ Yogurt of all sorts and makings

9. Automatic Cooking

It provides a fully automated process of cooking by timing each step of the task. The Instant Pot cooker can switch automatically from preheating to the cook cycle. Once the cooking is complete, it switches to "Keep Warm." This automatic cooking is greatly beneficial because you do not need to keep watching the cooking timer or monitoring the temperature levels. You do not have to be frequenting your kitchen to make your meal come out fine. You do not have to worry about overcooking. The Instant Pot comes with sensors for temperature and the pressure levels and it has other self-regulating features.

Though you have a 7-in-1 appliance, it is not so complicated to use. The automated cooking is activated with a few buttons to use with an understanding of a few basic tips.

10. Planning Meals With Delayed Cooking Made Easy

The Instant Pot can delay your cooking for up to 24 hours while your ingredient will not lose any part of its taste or spoil. That means you can set it to start cooking much later; for as long as a day. This is a great asset for a perfect meal planning. It is also cool for foods that are not in their best when frozen or refrigerated—beans, potatoes, rice and so on.

It also has short-term delay such that it can start your cooking in less than 2 hours which is also great for meal prepping. For instance, by reprogramming your main course, you have freed a lot of time to spend in preparing appetizers, desserts, and sides. Again, it affords you the opportunity to produce a tasty and healthy meal while not physically present in the kitchen.

11. It Aids Tenderness and Taste of Meats

When it comes to cooking those tougher cuts of meat, the Instant Pot cooking does it better than any other. It breaks down tough proteins and intramuscular fats quickly so that the meat can easily fall off the bone and eating is no struggle. Beans and legumes that can take all the time to get cooked can also be firmly cooked in reduced space of time.

12. It Cooks in a Clean and Pleasant Way

You do not have any struggle with a rattling steam-spewing monsters pot. The Instant Pot cooking is sleek and almost inaudible during cooking. It locks in aromas and flavors as observed, so your visitors hardly have an idea of when and what you are cooking. And it keeps your kitchen clean firstly, by reducing the number of appliances, and secondly by not spilling or spewing smokes.

13. No Need to Defrost In Microwave

Frozen foods cooked in the Instant Pot do not need defrosting. You, therefore do not need microwaving or wait for some time for your meat to defrost before you start cooking. Just toss them straight into the Instant Pot and there you go! In just a moment, you have finished a delicious meal.

Lightning Source UK Ltd.
Milton Keynes UK
UKHW050100050521
383095UK00002B/149